PENGUIN BOOKS — GREAT IDEAS

One Swallow Does Not Make a Summer

CW00952052

Aristotle

384–322 BC

Aristotle

*One Swallow Does Not
Make a Summer*

Translated by J. A. K. Thomson and Hugh Tredennick

PENGUIN BOOKS — GREAT IDEAS

PENGUIN BOOKS

UK | USA | Canada | Ireland | Australia
India | New Zealand | South Africa

Penguin Books is part of the Penguin Random House group
of companies whose addresses can be found at
global.penguinrandomhouse.com.

Penguin
Random House
UK

Originally published in *The Nicomachean Ethics*, translated by
J. A. K. Thomson, revised by Hugh Tredennick, Penguin Classics 2004
This selection published in Penguin Books 2020

Set in 10.25/12.75 pt Dante MT Std
Typeset by Jouve (UK), Milton Keynes
Printed and bound in Great Britain by Clays Ltd, Elcograf S.p.A.

A CIP catalogue record for this book
is available from the British Library

ISBN: 978-0-241-47286-6

www.greenpenguin.co.uk

MIX
Paper from
responsible sources
FSC® C018179

Penguin Random House is committed to a
sustainable future for our business, our readers
and our planet. This book is made from Forest
Stewardship Council® certified paper.

Contents

1 *The Object of Life*

*Every rational activity aims at some end or
good. One end (like one activity) may
be subordinate to another*

Every art and every investigation, and similarly every action
and pursuit, is considered to aim at some good. Hence the
good has been rightly defined as 'that at which all things
aim'. Clearly, however, there is some difference between the
ends at which they aim: some are activities and others results
distinct from the activities. Where there are ends distinct
from the actions, the results are by nature superior to the
activities. Since there are many actions, arts and sciences, it
follows that their ends are many too – the end of medical
science is health; of military science, victory; of economic
science, wealth. In the case of all skills of this kind that come
under a single faculty – as a skill in making bridles or any
other part of a horse's trappings comes under horsemanship,
while this and every kind of military action comes under
military science, so in the same way other skills are subordinate to yet others – in all these the ends of the directive
arts are to be preferred in every case to those of the subordinate ones, because it is for the sake of the former that
the latter are pursued also. It makes no difference whether
the ends of the actions are the activities themselves or

something apart from them, as in the case of the sciences we have mentioned.

If, then, our activities have some end which we want for its own sake, and for the sake of which we want all the other ends – if we do not choose everything for the sake of something else (for this will involve an infinite progression, so that our aim will be pointless and ineffectual) – it is clear that this must be the good, that is, the supreme good. Does it not follow, then, that a knowledge of the good is of great importance to us for the conduct of our lives? Are we not more likely to achieve our aim if we have a target? If this is so, we must try to describe at least in outline what the good really is, and by which of the sciences or faculties it is studied.

II.
The science that studies the supreme good for man is politics

Presumably this would be the most authoritative and directive science. Clearly this description fits the science of politics; for it is political science that prescribes what subjects are to be taught in states, and which of these the different sections of the community are to learn and up to what point. We see also that under this science come those faculties which are most highly esteemed; e.g. the arts of war, of property management and of public speaking. But if politics makes use of the other sciences, and also lays down what we should do and from what we should refrain, its end must include theirs; and this end must be the good for man. For even if the good of the community coincides with that of the individual, it is clearly a greater and more perfect thing to achieve and preserve that of a community; for while it is desirable to secure what is good in the case of an individual, to do so in the case of a people or a state is something finer and more sublime.

Such, then, is the aim of our investigation; and it is a kind of political science.

III.
Politics is not an exact science

Our account of this science will be adequate if it achieves such clarity as the subject-matter allows; for the same degree of precision is not to be expected in all discussions, any more than in all the products of handicraft. Instances of morally fine and just conduct – which is what politics investigates – involve so much difference and variety that they are widely believed to be such only by convention and not by nature. Instances of goods involve a similar kind of variety, for the reason that they often have hurtful consequences. People have been destroyed before now by their money, and others by their courage. Therefore in discussing subjects and arguing from evidence, conditioned in this way, we must be satisfied with a broad outline of the truth; that is, in arguing about what is for the most part so from premises which are for the most part true we must be content to draw conclusions that are similarly qualified. The same procedure, then, should be observed in receiving our several types of statement; for it is a mark of the trained mind never to expect more precision in the treatment of any subject than the nature of that subject permits; for demanding logical demonstrations from a teacher of rhetoric is clearly about as reasonable as accepting mere plausibility from a mathematician.

The student should have some general knowledge and experience of life

Since in every case a man judges rightly what he understands, and of this only is a good critic, it follows that while in a special field the good critic is a specialist, the good critic in general is the man with a general education. That is why a young man is not a fit person to attend lectures on political science, because he is not versed in the practical business of life from which politics draws its premises and subject-matter. Besides, he tends to follow his feelings, with the result that he will make no headway and derive no benefit from his course, since the object of it is not knowledge but action. It makes no difference whether he is young in age or youthful in character; the defect is due not to lack of years but to living, and pursuing one's various aims, under sway of the feelings; for to people like this knowledge becomes as unprofitable as it is for the incontinent. On the other hand for those who regulate their impulses and act in accordance with principle a knowledge of these subjects will be of great advantage.

So much by way of introductory remarks about the student, the proper attitude towards instruction, and the proposed course.

IV.
The end is no doubt happiness, but views of happiness differ

To resume. Since all knowledge and every pursuit aim at some good, what do we take to be the end of political science – what is the highest of all practical goods? Well, so far as the name goes there is pretty general agreement. 'It is happiness,' say both ordinary and cultured people; and they identify happiness with living well or doing well. But when it comes to saying in what happiness consists, opinions differ, and the account given by the generality of mankind is not at all like that of the wise. The former take it to be something obvious and familiar, like pleasure or money or eminence, and there are various other views; and often the same person actually changes his opinion: when he falls ill he says that it is health, and when he is hard up that it is money. Conscious of their own ignorance, most people are impressed by anyone who pontificates and says something that is over their heads. Some, however, have held the view that over and above these particular goods there is another which is good in itself and the cause of whatever goodness there is in all these others. It would no doubt be rather futile to examine all these opinions; enough if we consider those which are most prevalent or seem to have something to be said for them.

Learners must start from beliefs that are accepted or at least familiar

We must not overlook the difference that it makes whether we argue *from* or *to* first principles. Plato too used very properly to raise this question, inquiring whether the procedure was from or to first principles – just as on a race-track they run either from the judges' stand to the far end, or in the reverse direction. We must start from what is known. But things are known in two senses: known to us and known absolutely. Presumably *we* must start from what is known to us. So if anyone wants to make a serious study of ethics, or of political science generally, he must have been well trained in his habits. For the starting-point is the *fact*; and if this is sufficiently clear there will be no need to ascertain the reason why. Such a person can easily grasp the first principles if he is not in possession of them already; but one who has neither of these qualifications had better take to heart what Hesiod says:

> That man is best who sees the truth himself;
> Good too is he who listens to wise counsel.
> But who is neither wise himself nor willing
> To ponder wisdom is not worth a straw.

v.
The three types of life. Neither pleasure nor public honour seems to be an adequate end; the contemplative life will be considered later

But let us resume from the point at which we digressed. To judge by their lives, the masses and the most vulgar seem – not unreasonably – to believe that the good or happiness is pleasure. Accordingly they ask for nothing better than the life of enjoyment. (Broadly speaking, there are three main types of life: the one just mentioned, the political and, thirdly, the contemplative.) The utter servility of the masses comes out in their preference for a bovine existence; still, their view obtains consideration from the fact that many of those who are in positions of power share the tastes of Sardanapalus. Cultured people, however, and men of affairs identify the good with honour, because this is (broadly speaking) the goal of political life. Yet it appears to be too superficial to be the required answer. Honour is felt to depend more on those who confer than on him who receives it; and we feel instinctively that the good is something proper to its possessor and not easily taken from him. Again, people seem to seek honour in order to convince themselves of their own goodness; at any rate it is by intelligent men, and in a community where they are known, and for their goodness, that they seek to be honoured; so evidently in their view goodness is superior to honour. One might even be inclined to suppose that goodness rather than honour is the end pursued in public life. But even this appears to be somewhat deficient as an end, because the possession of goodness is thought to be compatible even with being asleep, or with leading a life of inactivity, and also with incurring the most atrocious suffering and misfortune; and nobody would call such a life happy – unless he was defending a paradox. So much for these views: they have been fully treated in current discussions. The third type of life is the contemplative, and this we shall examine later.

As for the life of the businessman, it does not give him much freedom of action. Besides, wealth is obviously not the good that we are seeking, because it serves only as a means; i.e. for getting something else. Hence the earlier suggestions might be supposed to be more likely ends, because they are appreciated on their own account; but evidently they too are inadequate, and many attacks on them have been published. Let them therefore be dismissed.

VI.
There cannot be a universal good such as Plato held to be the culmination of his theory of forms

Perhaps we had better examine the universal, and consider critically what is meant by it; although such a course is awkward, because the forms were introduced by friends of ours.

Yet surely it would be thought better, or rather necessary (above all for philosophers), to refute, in defence of the truth, even views to which one is attached; since although both are dear, it is right to give preference to the truth.

Those who introduced this theory did not posit ideas of classes in which they recognized degrees of priority (which also accounts for their not attempting to construct a form in the case of numbers). But things are called good both in the category of substance and in that of quality and in that of relation; and what exists in its own right, namely substance, is by nature prior to what is relative (for this is a sort of off-shoot or attribute of that which exists); so that there cannot be any common idea in these cases.

Again, things are called good in as many senses as they are said to exist; for they are so called in the category of substance (e.g. god or mind) and in quality (the virtues) and in quantity (what is moderate) and in relation (what is useful) and in time (opportunity) and in place (habitat) and so on. Clearly, then, there cannot be a single universal common to all cases, because it would be predicated not in all the categories but in one only.

Again, since of the things that come under one idea there is one single science, there would be some one science of all good things; but in fact there are more than one even of those that fall under one category: e.g. of opportunity, because in war it is the concern of military but in disease the concern of medical science; and of moderation, which in diet is the concern of medical science but in exercise the concern of physical training.

One might raise the question: What on earth do they mean by speaking of a thing-itself? – assuming that the definition of man is one and the same both in man and in man-himself; for *qua* man they will not differ at all, and if they do not, neither will what is good and the good-itself differ *qua* good. Nor will the good be any more good by being eternal, if a long-lasting white thing is no whiter than an ephemeral one. On this point the Pythagoreans (followed apparently by Speusippus) seem to have a more plausible doctrine, for they place unity in their column of goods. But we must leave the discussion of this to another occasion.

To the arguments that we have been using the objection presents itself that their statements do not apply to *every* good: that only those goods that are pursued or esteemed in their own right are called good in virtue of one form; those that are merely in some sense productive or conservative of these, or preventative of their contraries, are called good because of them and in a different sense. Clearly, then, things can be called good in two senses: some as good in their own right, and others as means to secure these. Let us, then, separate the things that are good in themselves from those that are merely useful, and consider whether they are called good in virtue of one idea. What sort of things can one posit as good in themselves? Everything that is pursued even when considered in isolation – intelligence, for example, and sight, and some pleasures and honours? for these are things which, even if we do pursue them on account of something else, nevertheless might be classed as good in themselves. Or nothing else at all except the idea? – then the class will be purposeless. If on the other hand the things that we have mentioned are also among those good in themselves, the definition of good will have to be recognizably the same in them all, just as that of white is in snow and chalk. But when it comes to honour and intelligence and pleasure, their definitions are different and distinct in respect of goodness.

Therefore good is not a common characteristic corresponding to one idea.

But in what sense, then, are these things called good?
because they do not seem to be accidental homonyms. Is it
that all goods derive from or contribute to one good? Or is
it rather that they are good by analogy: as sight is good in the
body, so is intuition in the mind, and so on? But perhaps this
subject should be dismissed here, since a detailed examination of it would be more appropriate for another branch of
philosophy. Similarly too with the idea of the good; for even
if the goodness that is predicated in common is some one
thing or has a separate existence of its own, clearly it cannot
be realized in action or acquired by man. Yet it is precisely
that sort of good that we are looking for now. It may perhaps
be thought that we had better gain knowledge of the good
as a means of attaining to those goods that *can* be acquired
and realized in practice; because if we have it as a pattern we
shall gain a better knowledge of the things that are good *for
us*, and so knowing, obtain them. The argument has a certain
plausibility, but it seems to clash with the procedure of the
practical sciences; for all these, though aiming at some good
and seeking to supply its deficiency, neglect knowledge of it.
Yet that all craftsmen should ignore such a potent aid and not
even try to secure it is not reasonable. And there is another
problem. What advantage in his art will a weaver or a joiner
get from knowledge of this good-itself? Or how will one who
has had a vision of the idea itself become thereby a better
doctor or general? As a matter of fact it does not appear that
the doctor even studies health in this way; his concern is the
health of a human being, or perhaps rather of a particular
patient, because what he treats is the individual. So much for
our discussion of this topic.

VII.

What is the good for man? It must be the ultimate end or object of human life: something that is in itself completely satisfying. Happiness fits this description

Let us now turn back again to the good which is the object of our search, and ask what it can possibly be; because it appears to vary with the action or art. It is one thing in medicine and another in strategy, and similarly in all the other sciences. What, then, is the good of each particular one? Surely it is that for the sake of which everything else is done. In medicine this is health; in strategy, victory; in architecture, a building – different things in different arts, but in every action and pursuit it is the *end*, since it is for the sake of this that everything else is done. Consequently if there is any one thing that is the end of all actions, this will be the practical good – or goods, if there are more than one. Thus while changing its ground the argument has reached the same conclusion as before.

We must try, however, to make our meaning still clearer. Since there are evidently more ends than one, and of these we choose some (e.g. wealth or musical instruments or tools generally) as means to something else, it is clear that not all of them are final ends, whereas the supreme good is obviously something final. So if there is only one final end, this will be the good of which we are in search; and if there are more than one, it will be the most final of these. Now we call an object pursued for its own sake more final than one pursued because of something else, and one which is never choosable because of another more final than those which are choosable because of it as well as for their own sakes; and that which is always choosable for its own sake and never because of something else we call final without any qualification.

Well, happiness more than anything else is thought to be just such an end, because we always choose it for itself, and never for any other reason. It is different with honour, pleasure, intelligence and good qualities generally. We do choose them partly for themselves (because we should choose each one of them irrespectively of any consequences); but we choose them also for the sake of our happiness, in the belief that they will be instrumental in promoting it. On the other hand nobody chooses happiness for *their* sake, or in general for any other reason.

The same conclusion seems to follow from another consideration. It is a generally accepted view that the perfect good is self-sufficient. By self-sufficient we mean not what is sufficient for oneself alone living a solitary life, but something that includes parents, wife and children, friends and fellow-citizens in general; for man is by nature a social being. (We must set some limit to these, for if we extend the application to grandparents and grandchildren and friends of friends it will proceed to infinity; but we must consider this point later.) A self-sufficient thing, then, we take to be one which by itself makes life desirable and in no way deficient; and we believe that happiness is such a thing. What is more, we regard it as the most desirable of all things, not reckoned as one item among many; if it were so reckoned, happiness would obviously be more desirable by the addition of even the least good, because the addition makes the sum of goods greater, and the greater of two goods is always more desirable. Happiness, then, is found to be something perfect and self-sufficient, being the end to which our actions are directed.

*But what is happiness? If we consider what
the function of man is, we find that happiness
is a virtuous activity of the soul*

But presumably to say that happiness is the supreme good
seems a platitude, and some more distinctive account of it is
still required. This might perhaps be achieved by grasping
what is the function of man. If we take a flautist or a sculptor
or any artist – or in general any class of men who have a specific function or activity – his goodness and proficiency are
considered to lie in the performance of that function; and the
same will be true of man, assuming that man has a function.
But is it likely that whereas joiners and shoemakers have
certain functions or activities, man as such has none, but has
been left by nature a functionless being? Just as we can see
that eye and hand and foot and every one of our members
have some function, should we not assume that in like manner a human being has a function over and above these
particular functions? What, then, can this possibly be? Clearly
life is a thing shared also by plants, and we are looking for
man's *proper* function; so we must exclude from our definition the life that consists in nutrition and growth. Next in
order would be a sort of sentient life; but this too we see is
shared by horses and cattle and animals of all kinds. There
remains, then, a practical life of the rational part. (This has
two aspects: one amenable to reason, the other possessing it
and initiating thought.) As this life also has two meanings,
we must lay down that we intend here life determined by
activity, because this is accepted as the stricter sense. Now,
if the function of man is an activity of the soul in accordance
with, or implying, a rational principle; and if we hold that the

function of an individual and of a good individual of the same kind – e.g. of a harpist and of a good harpist and so on generally – is generically the same, the latter's distinctive excellence being attached to the name of the function (because the function of the harpist is to play the harp, but that of the good harpist is to play it well); and if we assume that the function of man is a kind of life, namely, an activity or series of actions of the soul, implying a rational principle; and if the function of a good man is to perform these well and rightly; and if every function is performed well when performed in accordance with its proper excellence: if all this is so, the conclusion is that the good for man is an activity of the soul in accordance with virtue, or if there are more kinds of virtue than one, in accordance with the best and most perfect kind.

There is a further qualification: in a complete lifetime. One swallow does not make a summer; neither does one day. Similarly neither can one day, or a brief space of time, make a man blessed and happy.

This sketch can be elaborated later, but great precision is not to be expected

This may stand as an outline account of the good; for presumably we should first rough out a sketch and then fill in the details afterwards. When the outline has been satisfactorily drawn, it may be supposed that anybody can carry on the work and fill in the detail; and that in such a case time is a good source of invention or cooperation. In fact this is how progress in the arts has been made; for anyone can fill in the gaps. But we must still remember the caution given above, and not look for the same degree of exactness in all our studies, but only for as much as the subject-matter in each case allows and so far as is appropriate to the investigation. For example, a carpenter's interest in the right angle is different from a geometrician's: the former is concerned with it only so far as it is useful for his work, but the other wants to know what it is or what its properties are, because his gaze is set on the truth. We ought to follow this procedure in other studies as well, in order to prevent the swamping of main by side issues.

We must not even demand to know the explanation in all cases alike; there are some in which it is quite enough if the *fact* itself is exhibited, e.g. in the case of first principles; the fact is primary and a starting-point. Some starting-points are grasped by induction, some by perception, some by a kind of habituation, others in other ways. We must try to investigate each type in accordance with its nature. We must also make a point of formulating them correctly, because they have a great importance for the understanding of what follows. By common consent the beginning is more than half the whole task, and throws a flood of light on many of the aspects of the inquiry.

VIII.
Our view of happiness is supported by popular beliefs

We must examine our principle not only as reached logically, from a conclusion and premises, but also in the light of what is commonly said about it; because if a statement is true all the data are in harmony with it, while if it is false they soon reveal a discrepancy.

Now goods have been classified under three heads, as (1) external, (2) of the soul and (3) of the body. Of these we say that goods of the soul are good in the strictest and fullest sense, and we rank actions and activities of soul as goods of the soul; so that according to this view, which is of long standing and accepted by philosophers, our definition will be correct. We are right, too, in saying that the end consists in certain actions or activities, because this puts it among goods of the soul and not among external goods. Our definition is also supported by the belief that the happy man lives and fares well; because what we have described is virtually a kind of good life or prosperity. Again, our definition seems to include all the required constituents of happiness; for some think that it is virtue, others prudence and others wisdom; others that it is these or one of these, with the addition of pleasure, or not in total separation from it; and others further include favourable external conditions. Some of these views are popular beliefs of long standing; others are those of a few distinguished men. It is reasonable to suppose that neither group is entirely mistaken, but is right in some respect or even in most.

Now our definition is in harmony with those who say that happiness is virtue, or a particular virtue; because an activity in accordance with virtue implies virtue. But presumably it makes no little difference whether we think of the supreme good as consisting in the *possession* or in the *exercise* of virtue: in a state of mind or in an activity. For it is possible for the *state* to be present in a person without effecting any good result (e.g. if he is asleep or quiescent in some other way), but not for the *activity:* he will necessarily act, and act well. Just as at the Olympic Games it is not the best-looking or the strongest men present that are crowned with wreaths, but the competitors (because it is from them that the winners come), so it is those who *act* that rightly win the honours and rewards in life.

Moreover, the life of such people is in itself pleasant. For pleasure is an experience of the soul, and each individual finds pleasure in that of which he is said to be fond. For example, a horse gives pleasure to one who is fond of horses, and a spectacle to one who is fond of sight-seeing. In the same way just acts give pleasure to a lover of justice, and virtuous conduct generally to the lover of virtue. Now most people find that the things which give them pleasure conflict, because they are not pleasant by nature; but lovers of beauty find pleasure in things that are pleasant by nature, and virtuous actions are of this kind, so that they are pleasant not only to this type of person but also in themselves. So their life does not need to have pleasure attached to it as a sort of accessory, but contains its own pleasure in itself. Indeed, we may go further and assert that anyone who does not delight in fine actions is not even a good man; for nobody would say that a man is just unless he enjoys acting justly, nor liberal unless he enjoys liberal actions, and similarly in all the other cases. If this is so, virtuous actions must be pleasurable in themselves. What is more, they are both good and fine, and each in the highest degree, assuming that the good man is right in his judgement of them; and his judgement is as we have described. So happiness is the best, the finest, the most pleasurable thing of all; and these qualities are not separated as the inscription at Delos suggests:

Justice is loveliest, and health is best,
But sweetest to obtain is heart's desire.

All these attributes belong to the best activities; and it is these, or the one that is best of them, that we identify with happiness.

Nevertheless it seems clear that happiness needs the

addition of external goods, as we have said; for it is difficult if not impossible to do fine deeds without any resources. Many can only be done as it were by instruments – by the help of friends, or wealth, or political influence. There are also certain advantages, such as good ancestry or good children or personal beauty, the lack of which mars our felicity; for a man is scarcely happy if he is very ugly to look at, or of low birth, or solitary and childless; and presumably even less so if he has children or friends who are quite worthless, or if he had good ones who are now dead. So, as we said, happiness seems to require this sort of prosperity too; which is why some identify it with good fortune, although others identify it with virtue.

IX.
How is happiness acquired?

From this springs another problem. Is happiness something that can be learnt, or acquired by habituation or cultivated in some other way, or does it come to us by a sort of divine dispensation or even by chance? Well, in the first place, if anything is a gift of the gods to men, it is reasonable that happiness should be such a gift, especially since of all human possessions it is the best. This point, however, would perhaps be considered more appropriately by another branch of study. Yet even if happiness is not sent by a divine power, but is acquired by moral goodness and by some kind of study or training, it seems clearly to be one of our most divine possessions; for the crown and end of goodness is surely of all things the best: something divine and blissful. Also on this view happiness will be something widely shared; for it can attach, through some form of study or application, to anyone who is not handicapped by some incapacity for goodness. And, assuming that it is better to win happiness by the means described than by chance, it is reasonable that this should in fact be so, since it is natural for nature's effects to be the finest possible, and similarly for the effects of art and of any other cause, especially those of the best kind. That the most import-ant and finest thing of all should be left to chance would be a gross disharmony.

The problem also receives some light from our definition, for in it happiness has been described as a kind of virtuous activity of soul; whereas all the other goods either are neces-sary preconditions of happiness or naturally contribute to it and serve as its instruments. This will agree with what we said at the outset: we suggested that the end of political sci-ence is the highest good; and the chief concern of this science is to endue the citizens with certain qualities, namely virtue and the readiness to do fine deeds. Naturally, therefore, we do not speak of an ox or a horse or any other animal as happy, because none of them can take part in this sort of activity. For the same reason no child is happy either, because its age debars it as yet from such activities; if children are so described, it is by way of congratulation on their future prom-ise. For, as we said above, happiness demands not only complete goodness but a complete life. In the course of life we encounter many reverses and all kinds of vicissitudes, and in old age even the most prosperous of men may be involved in great misfortunes, as we are told about Priam in the Trojan poems. Nobody calls happy a man who suffered fortunes like his and met a miserable end.

x.

*Is it only when his life is completed that
a man can rightly be called happy?*

Ought we, then, to go further and call no man happy so long
as he is alive? Must we, in Solon's phrase, 'look to the end'?
And if we *are* bound to lay down this rule, is a man really
happy after he is dead? Surely this is an utter paradox, especially for us who define happiness as a kind of activity. On
the other hand if we deny that a dead man is happy – if Solon's
words mean something else, namely that only when a man
is dead can one safely congratulate him on being immune
from evil and misfortune – even this admits of some dispute;
for it is popularly believed that some good and evil – such as
honours and dishonours, and successes and disasters of his
children and descendants generally – can happen to a dead
man, inasmuch as they can happen to a live one without his
being aware of them. But this too entails a difficulty. Suppose
that a man has lived an exceptionally happy life right into old
age, and has ended it in like manner: many changes of fortune
may befall his descendants, some of whom may be good and
enjoy such a life as they deserve, and others just the opposite;
and they may of course be separated from their ancestors by
any number of generations. It would surely be absurd, then,
if the dead man changed with their changes of fortune, and
became at one time happy and then in turn miserable; but it
would also be absurd for the experiences of the descendants
to have no effect, even for a limited period, upon their
ancestors.

But let us return to the difficulty that we raised earlier;
because perhaps that will throw light on our present problem.

If we must 'look to the end' and only then call a man happy, not because he *is* but because he *was* so before, surely it will be absurd if when a man *is* happy the fact cannot be truly stated of him – for the reason that we are unwilling to call the living happy because of the changes of fortune, and because we have assumed that happiness is a permanent thing and not at all liable to change, whereas fortune's wheel often turns upside down for the same people! For clearly, supposing that we follow the guidance of his fortunes, we shall often call the same man by turns happy and miserable, representing the happy man as a sort of 'chameleon; a castle set on sand'. Probably it is not right at all to follow the changes of a man's fortunes, because success and failure in life do not depend on these; they are merely complements, as we said, of human life. It is virtuous activities that determine our happiness, and the opposite kind that produce the opposite effect.

Our examination of this problem bears out our definition, because no other human operation has the same permanence as virtuous activities (they are considered to be more persistent even than the several kinds of scientific knowledge); and of these themselves the most highly esteemed are more persistent than the rest, because it is in them that the truly happy most fully and continuously spend their lives: this seems to be the reason why we do not forget them. We conclude, then, that the happy man will have the required quality, and in fact will be happy throughout his life; because he will spend all his time, or the most time of any man, in virtuous conduct and contemplation. And he will bear his fortunes in the finest spirit and with perfect sureness of touch, as being 'good in very truth' and 'foursquare without reproach'.

Yet the accidents of fortune are many, and they vary in importance. Little pieces of good luck (and likewise of the opposite kind) clearly do not disturb the tenor of our life. On the other hand many great strokes of fortune, if favourable, will make life more felicitous (since they tend naturally of themselves to add to its attractions, and also they can be used in a fine and responsible way); but if they fall out adversely they restrict and spoil our felicity, both by inflicting pain and by putting a check on many of our activities. Nevertheless even here, when a man bears patiently a number of heavy disasters, not because he does not feel them but because he has a high and generous nature, his nobility shines through. And if, as we said, the quality of a life is determined by its activities, no man who is truly happy can become miserable; because he will never do things that are hateful and mean. For we believe that the truly good and wise man bears all his fortunes with dignity, and always takes the most honourable course that circumstances permit; just as a good general uses his available forces in the most militarily effective way, and a good shoemaker makes the neatest shoe out of the leather supplied to him, and the same with all the other kinds of craftsmen. And if this is so, the happy man can never become miserable – although he cannot be entirely happy if he falls in with fortunes like those of Priam. Nor indeed can he be variable and inconstant; for he will not be dislodged from his happiness easily nor by ordinary misfortunes – only by a succession of heavy blows, and from these he will not quickly recover his happiness; if he does so at all, it will only be at the end of a long interval in which he has attained great and splendid achievements.

We are now in a position to define the happy man as 'one who is active in accordance with complete virtue, and who is adequately furnished with external goods, and that not for some unspecified period but throughout a complete life'. And probably we should add 'destined both to live in this way and to die accordingly'; because the future is obscure to us, and happiness we maintain to be an *end* in every way utterly final and complete. If this is so, then we shall describe those of the living who possess and will continue to possess the stated qualifications as supremely happy – but with a human happiness.

So much for our systematic treatment of this subject.

XI.
Are the dead affected by the fortunes of those who survive them?

The notion that the dead are not affected at all by the fortunes of their descendants or any of those whom they love seems unduly heartless and contrary to accepted beliefs. But experiences are so many and exhibit such a variety of differences, some touching us more closely than others, that it would obviously be a long or rather an endless task to distinguish between them in detail; a general account in broad outline may perhaps be sufficient.

Since, then, a man's own misfortunes sometimes have a powerful influence upon his life, and sometimes seem comparatively trivial; and the same applies also to the misfortunes of all his friends alike; although it makes a difference whether a particular misfortune befalls people while they are alive or after they are dead – a far greater difference than it makes in a tragedy whether the crimes and atrocities are committed beforehand or carried out during the action; then we must take into our reckoning this difference too; or rather, perhaps, the fact that it is questionable whether the departed have any participation in good or its opposite. For the probable inference from what we have been saying is that if any effect of good or evil reaches them at all, it must be faint and slight, either in itself or to them – or if not that, at any rate not of such force and quality as to make the unhappy happy or to rob the happy of their felicity. So it appears that the dead are affected to some extent by the good fortunes of those whom they love, and similarly by their misfortunes; but that the effects are not of such a kind or so great as to make the happy unhappy, or to produce any other such result.

XII.
Is happiness to be praised as a means or valued as an end?

Now that we have decided these questions let us consider whether happiness is something that is *praised* or something that is *valued* (for it is clearly not a mere potentiality). Well, everything that we praise seems to be praised because it has a certain quality and stands in a certain relation to something else; for we praise the just man and the brave man, and in general the good man and virtue, because of the actions and effects that they produce; and we praise the strong and swift-footed and every other such type of man because he has a certain natural quality and stands in a certain relation to something good and worthwhile. This is evident also from the consideration of praise addressed to the gods: it is obviously absurd that the gods should be referred to our standards, yet this follows from the fact that (as we said) praise involves reference to something else. But if praise belongs to what is relative, clearly the best things call not for praise but for something greater and better, as in fact we find; because we call the gods 'happy' or 'blessed', a term which we apply also to such men as most closely resemble the gods. Similarly too with *things* that are good. No one praises happiness as he praises justice; he calls it 'blessed', as being something better and more divine. Eudoxus too is held to have made a good point in supporting the claim of pleasure to supremacy; he thought that the fact of its not being praised, although it is a good, is evidence that it is superior to the goods that are praised, as gods and the good are also, because they are the standards to which all other goods are referred. For praise is concerned with goodness, because this enables men to do fine deeds; while encomia are directed towards achievements, physical and non-physical alike. However, the detailed examination of this subject is presumably more appropriate for those who have made a special study of encomia. For us it is clear, from what has been said already, that happiness is one of those things that are precious and perfect. This view seems to be confirmed by the fact that it is a first principle, since everything else that any of us do, we do for its sake; and we hold that the first principle and cause of what is good is precious and divine.

XIII.

To understand what moral goodness is we must study the soul of man

Since happiness is an activity of the soul in accordance with perfect virtue, we must examine the nature of virtue; for perhaps in this way we shall be better able to form a view about happiness too. Besides, the true statesman is thought of as a man who has taken special pains to study this subject; for he wants to make his fellow-citizens good and law-abiding people (we have an example of this in the lawgivers of Crete and Sparta, and any others who have shown similar qualities). And if this investigation is a part of political science, clearly our inquiry will be in keeping with the plan that we adopted at the outset.

The goodness that we have to consider is human goodness, obviously; for it was the good *for man* or happiness *for man* that we set out to discover. But by human goodness is meant goodness not of the body but of the soul, and happiness also we define as an activity of the soul. This being so, it is evident that the statesman ought to have some acquaintance with psychology, just as a doctor who intends to treat the eye must have a knowledge of the body as a whole. Indeed the statesman's need is greater than the doctor's, inasmuch as politics is a better and more honourable science than medicine. But the best kind of doctors take a good deal of trouble to acquire a knowledge of the body; so the statesman too must study the soul, but with a view to politics, and only so far as is sufficient for the questions that we are investigating; for to explore its nature in greater detail would presumably be too laborious for our present purpose.

The several faculties of the soul distinguished

Some aspects of psychology are adequately treated in discourses elsewhere, and we should make use of the results: e.g. that the soul is part rational and part irrational (whether these are separate like the parts of the body or anything else that is physically divisible, or whether like the convex and concave aspects of the circumference of a circle they are distinguishable as two only in definition and thought, and are by nature inseparable, makes no difference for our present purpose). Of the irrational soul one part seems to be common, namely the vegetative: I mean the cause of nutrition and growth; because one can assume such a faculty of soul in everything that receives nourishment, even in embryos; and this same faculty too in the fully developed creature, because this is more reasonable than to suppose that the latter has a different one. Thus the excellence of this faculty is evidently common and not confined to man; because this part or faculty seems to be most active in sleep, when the good and the bad are least easy to distinguish (hence the saying 'for half their lives the happy are no different from the wretched'). This is a natural consequence, because sleep is a suspension of that function of the soul by which it is distinguished as good and bad – except that to a certain limited extent some of the stimuli reach the soul; this is what makes the dreams of decent people better than those of the ordinary man. But enough of this subject; we may dismiss the nutritive soul, because of its very nature it has no part in human goodness.

But there seems to be another element of the soul which, while irrational, is in a sense receptive of reason. Take the types of man which we call continent and incontinent. They have a principle – a rational element in their souls – which we commend, because it urges them in the right direction and encourages them to take the best course; but there is also observable in them another element, by nature irrational, which struggles and strains against the rational. Just as in the case of the body paralysed limbs, when the subject chooses to move them to the right, swing away in the contrary direction to the left, so exactly the same happens in the case of the soul; for the impulses of the incontinent take them in the contrary direction. 'But in bodies we see what swings away, whereas in the case of the soul we do not.' Probably we should believe nevertheless that the soul too contains an irrational element which opposes and runs counter to reason – in what sense it is a separate element does not matter at all. But this too, as we said, seems to be receptive of reason; at any rate in the continent man it is obedient to reason, and is presumably still more amenable in the temperate and in the brave man, because in them it is in complete harmony with the rational principle.

Evidently, then, the irrational part of the soul also consists of two parts. The vegetative has no association at all with reason, but the desiderative and generally appetitive part does in a way participate in reason, in the sense that it is submissive and obedient to it (this is the sense of *logon echein* in which we speak of 'taking account' of one's father or friends, not that in which we speak of 'having an account' of mathematical propositions). That the irrational part is in some way persuaded by reason is indicated by our use of admonition, and of reproof and encouragement of all kinds. If, however, one should speak of the appetitive part of the soul as rational too, it will be the rational part that is divided in two: one rational in the proper sense of the word and in itself, the other in the sense that a child pays attention to its father.

Virtue, too, is divided into classes in accordance with this differentiation of the soul. Some virtues are called intellectual and others moral; wisdom and understanding and prudence are intellectual, liberality and temperance are moral virtues. When we are speaking of a man's *character* we do not describe him as wise or understanding, but as patient or temperate. We do, however, praise a wise man on the ground of his state of mind; and those states that are praiseworthy we call virtues.

II *Moral Goodness*

I.
Moral virtues, like crafts, are acquired by practice and habituation

Virtue, then, is of two kinds, intellectual and moral. Intellectual virtue owes both its inception and its growth chiefly to instruction, and for this very reason needs time and experience. Moral goodness, on the other hand, is the result of habit, from which it has actually got its name, being a slight modification of the word *ethos*. This fact makes it obvious that none of the moral virtues is engendered in us by nature, since nothing that is what it is by nature can be made to behave differently by habituation. For instance, a stone, which has a natural tendency downwards, cannot be habituated to rise, however often you try to train it by throwing it into the air; nor can you train fire to burn downwards; nor can anything else that has any other natural tendency be trained to depart from it. The moral virtues, then, are engendered in us neither *by* nor *contrary to* nature; we are constituted by nature to receive them, but their full development in us is due to habit.

Again, of all those faculties with which nature endows us we first acquire the potentialities, and only later effect their actualization. (This is evident in the case of the senses. It was not from repeated acts of seeing or hearing that we acquired the senses but the other way round: we had these senses before we used them; we did not acquire them as the result of using them.) But the virtues we do acquire by first exercising them, just as happens in the arts. Anything that we have to learn to do we learn by the actual doing of it: people become builders by building and instrumentalists by playing instruments. Similarly we become just by performing just acts, temperate by performing temperate ones, brave by performing brave ones. This view is supported by what happens in city-states. Legislators make their citizens good by habituation; this is the intention of every legislator, and those who do not carry it out fail of their object. This is what makes the difference between a good constitution and a bad one.

Again, the causes or means that bring about any form of excellence are the same as those that destroy it, and similarly with art; for it is as a result of playing the harp that people become good and bad harpists. The same principle applies to builders and all other craftsmen. Men will become good builders as a result of building well, and bad ones as a result of building badly. Otherwise there would be no need of anyone to teach them: they would all be *born* either good or bad. Now this holds good also of the virtues. It is the way that we behave in our dealings with other people that makes us just or unjust, and the way that we behave in the face of danger, accustoming ourselves to be timid or confident, that makes us brave or cowardly. Similarly with situations involving desires and angry feelings: some people become temperate and patient from one kind of conduct in such situations, others licentious and choleric from another. In a word, then, like activities produce like dispositions. Hence we must give our activities a certain quality, because it is their characteristics that determine the resulting dispositions. So it is a matter of no little importance what sort of habits we form from the earliest age – it makes a vast difference, or rather all the difference in the world.

II.

In a practical science so much depends upon particular circumstances that only general rules can be given

Since the branch of philosophy on which we are at present engaged is not, like the others, theoretical in its aim – because we are studying not to know what goodness is, but how to become good men, since otherwise it would be useless – we must apply our minds to the problem of how our actions should be performed, because, as we have just said, it is these that actually determine our dispositions.

Now, that we should act according to the right principle is common ground and may be assumed as a basis for discussion (the point will be discussed later, both what 'the right principle' is, and how it is related to the other virtues). But we must first agree that any account of conduct must be stated in outline and not in precise detail, just as we said at the beginning that accounts are to be required only in such a form as befits their subject-matter. Now questions of conduct and expedience have as little fixity about them as questions of what is healthful; and if this is true of the general rule, it is still more true that its application to particular problems admits of no precision. For they do not fall under any art or professional tradition, but the agents are compelled at every step to think out for themselves what the circumstances demand, just as happens in the arts of medicine and

navigation. However, although our present account is of this
kind, we must try to support it.

A cardinal rule: right conduct is incompatible with excess or deficiency in feelings and actions

First, then, we must consider this fact: that it is in the nature
of moral qualities that they are destroyed by deficiency and
excess, just as we can see (since we have to use the evidence
of visible facts to throw light on those that are invisible) in
the case of health and strength. For both excessive and insuf-
ficient exercise destroy one's strength, and both eating and
drinking too much or too little destroy health, whereas the
right quantity produces, increases and preserves it. So it is
the same with temperance, courage and the other virtues.
The man who shuns and fears everything and stands up to
nothing becomes a coward; the man who is afraid of nothing
at all, but marches up to every danger, becomes foolhardy.
Similarly the man who indulges in every pleasure and
refrains from none becomes licentious; but if a man behaves
like a boor and turns his back on every pleasure, he is a case
of insensibility. Thus temperance and courage are destroyed
by excess and deficiency and preserved by the mean.

Our virtues are exercised in the same kinds of action as gave rise to them

But besides the fact that the virtues are induced and fostered as
a result, and by the agency, of the same sort of actions as cause
their destruction, the activities that flow from them will also
consist in the same sort of actions. This is so in all the other
more observable instances, e.g. in that of strength. This results

from taking plenty of nourishment and undergoing severe training, and it is the strong man that will be best able to carry out this programme. So with the virtues. It is by refraining from pleasures that we become temperate, and it is when we have become temperate that we are most able to abstain from pleasures. Similarly with courage; it is by habituating ourselves to make light of alarming situations and to face them that we become brave, and it is when we have become brave that we shall be most able to face an alarming situation.

III.

*The pleasure or pain that actions cause the
agent may serve as an index of moral progress,
since good conduct consists in a proper
attitude towards pleasure and pain*

The pleasure or pain that accompanies people's acts should be taken as a sign of their dispositions. A man who abstains from bodily pleasures and enjoys the very fact of so doing is temperate; if he finds it irksome he is licentious. Again, the man who faces danger gladly, or at least without distress, is brave; the one who feels distressed is a coward. For it is with pleasures and pains that moral goodness is concerned. Pleasure induces us to behave badly, and pain to shrink from fine actions. Hence the importance (as Plato says) of having been trained in some way from infancy to feel joy and grief at the right things: true education is precisely this. If the virtues are concerned with actions and feelings, and every feeling and every action is always accompanied by pleasure or pain, on this ground too virtue will be concerned with pleasures and pains. The fact that punishments are effected by their means is further evidence, because punishment is a kind of remedial treatment, and such treatment is naturally effected by contraries. Again, as we said above, every state of the soul attains its natural development in relation to, and in the sphere of, those conditions by which it is naturally made better or worse. Now when people become bad it is because of pleasures and pains, through seeking (or shunning) the wrong ones, or at the wrong time, or in the wrong way or in any other manner in which such offences are distinguished by principle. This is why some thinkers actually define the virtues as forms of impassivity or tranquillity. But they are wrong in speaking absolutely instead of adding 'in the right (or wrong) manner and at the right time' and any other due qualifications.

We have decided, then, that this kind of virtue disposes us to act in the best way with regard to pleasures and pains, and contrariwise with the corresponding vice. But we may obtain further light on the same point from the following considerations.

There are three factors that make for choice, and three that make for avoidance: the fine, the advantageous and the pleasant, and their contraries, the base, the harmful and the painful. Now, with regard to all these the good man tends to go right and the bad man to go wrong, especially about pleasure. This is common to all animals, and accompanies all objects of choice, for clearly the fine and the advantageous are pleasant too. Consciousness of pleasure has grown up with all of us from our infancy, and therefore our life is so deeply imbued with this feeling that it is hard to remove all trace of it. Pleasure and pain are also the standards by which – to a greater or lesser extent – we regulate our actions. Since to feel pleasure and pain rightly or wrongly has no little effect upon conduct, it follows that our whole inquiry must be concerned with these sensations. Heraclitus says that it is hard to fight against emotion, but harder still to fight against pleasure; and the harder course is always the concern of both art and virtue, because success is better in the face of difficulty. Thus on this ground too the whole concern of both morality and political science must be with pleasures and pains, since the man who treats them rightly will be good and the one who treats them wrongly will be bad.

We may take this as a sufficient statement that virtue is concerned with pains and pleasures; that the actions that produce it also increase it, or if differently performed, destroy it; and that the actions that produce it also constitute the sphere of its activity.

IV.

Acts that are incidentally virtuous distinguished
from those that are done knowingly, of choice
and from a virtuous disposition

A difficulty, however, may be raised as to how we can say that people must perform just actions if they are to become just, and temperate ones if they are to become temperate; because if they do what is just and temperate, they are just and temperate already, in the same way that if they use words or play music correctly they are already literate or musical. But surely this is not true even of the arts. It is possible to put a few words together correctly by accident, or at the prompting of another person; so the agent will only be literate if he does a literate act in a literate way, that is, in virtue of his own literacy. Nor, again, is there an analogy between the arts and the virtues. Works of art have their merit in themselves; so it is enough for them to be turned out with a certain quality of their own. But virtuous acts are not done in a just or temperate way merely because *they* have a certain quality, but only if the agent also acts in a certain state, that is, (1) if he knows what he is doing, (2) if he chooses it, and chooses it for its own sake, and (3) if he does it from a fixed and permanent disposition. Now these – knowledge excepted – are not reckoned as necessary qualifications for the arts as well. For the acquisition of virtues, on the other hand, knowledge has little or no force; but the other requirements are not of little but of supreme importance, granted that it is from the repeated performance of just and temperate acts that we acquire virtues. Acts, to be sure, are called just and temperate when they are such as a just or temperate man would do; but what makes the agent just or temperate is not merely the fact that he does such things, but the fact that he does them in the way that just and temperate men do. It is therefore right to say that a man becomes just by the performance of just, and temperate by the performance of temperate, acts; nor is there the smallest likelihood of any man's becoming good by not doing them. This is not, however, the course that most people follow: they have recourse to their principle, and imagine that they are being philosophical and that in this way they will become serious-minded – behaving rather like invalids who listen carefully to their doctor, but carry out none of his instructions. Just as the bodies of the latter will get no benefit from such treatment, so the souls of the former will get none from such philosophy.

v.

In order to define virtue we must decide to what
class or genus it belongs. It is not a feeling or
a faculty, but a disposition

We must now consider what virtue is. Since there are three kinds of modification that are found in the soul, namely feelings, faculties and dispositions, virtue must be one of these three. By feelings I mean desire, anger, fear, daring, envy, joy, friendliness, hatred, longing, jealousy, pity and in general all conditions that are attended by pleasure or pain. By faculties I mean those susceptibilities in virtue of which we are said to be capable of the feelings in question, e.g. capable of anger or sorrow or pity. By dispositions I mean conditions in virtue of which we are well or ill disposed in respect of the feelings concerned. We have, for instance, a bad disposition towards anger if our tendency is too strong or too weak, and a good one if our tendency is moderate. Similarly with the other feelings.

Now, neither the virtues nor the vices are feelings, because we are not called good or bad on the ground of our feelings, but we are so called on the ground of our virtues and vices; nor are we either praised or blamed for our feelings (a man is not praised for being frightened or angry, nor is he blamed just for being angry; it is for being angry in a particular way); but we *are* praised and blamed for our virtues and vices. Again, when we are angry or frightened it is not by our choice; but our virtues are expressions of our choice, or at any rate imply choice. Besides, we are said to be moved in respect of our feelings, but in respect of our virtues and vices we are said to be not moved but disposed in a particular way. By the same line of reasoning they are not faculties either. We are not called good or bad, nor are we praised or blamed, merely because we are *capable* of feeling. Again, what faculties we have, we have by nature; but it is not nature that makes us good or bad (we mentioned this point above). So if the virtues are neither feelings nor faculties, it remains that they are dispositions.

We have now stated what virtue is generically.

VI.

But what is its differentia? Any excellence enables
its possessor to function well; therefore this
is true of human excellence, i.e. virtue

But we must not only make the simple statement that it is a
disposition; we must also say what *kind* of disposition. Let us
assert, then, that any kind of excellence renders that of which
it is the excellence *good*, and makes it perform its function
well. For example, the excellence of the eye makes both the
eye and its function good (because it is through the excellence
of the eye that we see well). Similarly the excellence of a horse
makes him both a fine horse and good at running and carry-
ing his rider and facing the enemy. If this rule holds good for
all cases, then *human* excellence will be the disposition that
makes one a good man and causes him to perform his function well. We have already explained how this will be; but it
will also become clear in another way if we consider what is
the specific nature of virtue.

This is confirmed by the doctrine of the mean

In anything continuous and divisible it is possible to take a
part which is greater or less than, or equal to, the remainder;
and that in relation either to the thing divided or to us. The
equal part is a sort of mean between excess and deficiency;
and I call mean in relation to the *thing* whatever is equidistant
from the extremes, which is one and the same for everybody;
but I call mean in relation to *us* that which is neither excessive
nor deficient, and this is *not* one and the same for all. For
example, if ten is 'many' and two 'few' of some quantity, six

is the mean if one takes it in relation to the thing, because it exceeds the one number and is exceeded by the other by the same amount; and this is the mean by arithmetical reckoning. But the mean in relation to *us* is not to be obtained in this way. Supposing that ten pounds of food is a large and two pounds a small allowance for an athlete, it does not follow that the trainer will prescribe six pounds; for even this is perhaps too much or too little for the person who is to receive it – too little for Milo but too much for one who is only beginning to train. Similarly in the case of running and wrestling. In this way, then, every knowledgeable person avoids excess and deficiency, but looks for the mean and chooses it – not the mean of the thing, but the mean relative to us.

If, then, every science performs its function well only when it observes the mean and refers its products to it (which is why it is customary to say of well executed works that nothing can be added to them or taken away, the implication being that excess and deficiency alike destroy perfection, while the mean preserves it) – if good craftsmen, as we hold, work with the mean in view; and if virtue, like nature, is more exact and more efficient than any art, it follows that virtue aims to hit the mean. By virtue I mean moral virtue since it is this that is concerned with feelings and actions, and these involve excess, deficiency and a mean. It is possible, for example, to feel fear, confidence, desire, anger, pity, and pleasure and pain generally, too much or too little; and both of these are wrong. But to have these feelings at the right times on the right grounds towards the right people for the right motive and in the right way is to feel them to an intermediate, that is to the best, degree; and this is the mark of virtue. Similarly there are excess and deficiency and a mean

in the case of actions. But it is in the field of actions and feelings that virtue operates; and in them excess and deficiency
are failings, whereas the mean is praised and recognized as
a success: and these are both marks of virtue. Virtue, then,
is a mean condition, inasmuch as it aims at hitting the mean.

Again, failure is possible in many ways (for evil, as the
Pythagoreans represented it, is a form of the unlimited, and
good of the limited), but success in only one. That is why the
one is easy and the other difficult; it is easy to miss the target
and difficult to hit it. Here, then, is another reason why excess
and deficiency fall under evil, and the mean state under good;
'For men are bad in countless ways, but good in only one.'

A provisional definition of virtue

So virtue is a purposive disposition, lying in a mean that is
relative to us and determined by a rational principle, and by
that which a prudent man would use to determine it. It is a
mean between two kinds of vice, one of excess and the other
of deficiency; and also for this reason, that whereas these
vices fall short of or exceed the right measure in both feelings
and actions, virtue discovers the mean and chooses it. Thus
from the point of view of its essence and the definition of its
real nature, virtue is a mean; but in respect of what is right
and best, it is an extreme.

But the rule of choosing the mean cannot be applied to some actions and feelings, which are essentially evil

But not every action or feeling admits of a mean; because
some have names that directly connote depravity, such as
malice, shamelessness and envy, and among actions adultery,

theft and murder. All these, and more like them, are so called as being evil in themselves; it is not the excess or deficiency of them that is evil. In their case, then, it is impossible to act rightly; one is always wrong. Nor does acting rightly or wrongly in such cases depend upon circumstances – whether a man commits adultery with the right woman or at the right time or in the right way – because to do anything of that kind is simply wrong. One might as well claim that there is a mean and excess and deficiency even in unjust or cowardly or intemperate actions. On that basis there must be a mean of excess, a mean of deficiency, an excess of excess and a deficiency of deficiency. But just as in temperance and courage there can be no mean or excess or deficiency, because the mean is in a sense an extreme, so there can be no mean or excess or deficiency in the vices that we mentioned; however done, they are wrong. For in general neither excess nor deficiency admits of a mean, nor does a mean admit of excess and deficiency.

VII.
The doctrine of the mean applied to particular virtues

But a generalization of this kind is not enough; we must apply it to particular cases. When we are discussing actions, although general statements have a wider application, particular statements are closer to the truth. This is because actions are concerned with particular facts, and theories must be brought into harmony with these. Let us, then, take these instances from the diagram.

In the field of fear and confidence the mean is courage; and of those who go to extremes the man who exceeds in fearlessness has no name to describe him (there are many nameless cases), the one who exceeds in confidence is called rash, and the one who shows an excess of fear and a deficiency of confidence is called cowardly. In the field of pleasures and pains – not in all, especially not in all pains – the mean is temperance, the excess licentiousness; cases of defective response to pleasures scarcely occur, and therefore people of this sort too have no name to describe them, but let us class them as insensible. In the field of giving and receiving money the mean is liberality, the excess and deficiency are prodigality and illiberality; but these show excess and deficiency in contrary ways to one another: the prodigal man goes too far in spending and not far enough in getting, while the illiberal man goes too far in getting money and not far enough in spending it. This present account is in outline and summary, which is all that we need at this stage; we shall give a more accurate analysis later.

But there are other dispositions too that are concerned with money. There is a mean called magnificence (because the magnificent is not the same as the liberal man: the one deals in large and the other in small outlays); the excess is tastelessness and vulgarity, the deficiency pettiness. These are different from the extremes between which liberality lies; how they differ will be discussed later. In the field of honour and dishonour the mean is magnanimity, the excess is called a sort of vanity, and the deficiency pusillanimity. And just as liberality differs, as we said, from magnificence in being concerned with small outlays, so there is a state related to magnanimity in the same way, being concerned with small honours, while magnanimity is concerned with great ones; because it is possible to aspire to small honours in the right way, or to a greater or lesser degree than is right. The man who goes too far in his aspirations is called ambitious, the one who falls short, unambitious; the one who is a mean between them has no name. This is true also of the corresponding dispositions, except that the ambitious man's is called ambitiousness. This is why the extremes lay claim to the intermediate territory. We ourselves sometimes call the intermediate man ambitious and sometimes unambitious; that is, we sometimes commend the ambitious and sometimes the unambitious. Why it is that we do this will be explained in our later remarks. Meanwhile let us continue our discussion of the remaining virtues and vices, following the method already laid down.

In the field of anger, too, there is excess, deficiency and the mean. They do not really possess names, but we may call the intermediate man patient and the mean patience; and of the extremes the one who exceeds can be irascible and his vice irascibility, while the one who is deficient can be spiritless and the deficiency lack of spirit.

There are also three other means which, though different, somewhat resemble each other. They are all concerned with what we do and say in social intercourse, but they differ in this respect, that one is concerned with truthfulness in such intercourse, the other two with pleasantness – one with pleasantness in entertainment, the other with pleasantness in every department of life. We must therefore say something about these too, in order that we may better discern that in all things the mean is to be commended, while the extremes are neither commendable nor right, but reprehensible. Most of these too have no names; but, as in the other cases, we must try to coin names for them in the interest of clarity and to make it easy to follow the argument.

Well, then, as regards truth the intermediate man may be called truthful and the mean truthfulness; pretension that goes too far may be boastfulness and the man who is disposed to it a boaster, while that which is deficient may be called irony and its exponent ironical. As for pleasantness in social entertainment, the intermediate man is witty, and the disposition wit; the excess is buffoonery and the indulger in it a buffoon; the man who is deficient is a kind of boor and his disposition boorishness. In the rest of the sphere of the pleasant – life in general – the person who is pleasant in the right way is friendly and the mean is friendliness; the person who goes too far, if he has no motive, is obsequious; if his motive is self-interest, he is a flatterer. The man who is deficient and is unpleasant in all circumstances is cantankerous and ill-tempered.

There are mean states also in the sphere of feelings and emotions. Modesty is not a virtue, but the modest man too is praised. Here too one person is called intermediate and another excessive – like the shy man who is overawed at anything. The man who feels too little shame or none at all is shameless, and the intermediate man is modest. Righteous indignation is a mean between envy and spite, and they are all concerned with feelings of pain or pleasure at the experiences of our neighbours. The man who feels righteous indignation is distressed at instances of undeserved good fortune, but the envious man goes further and is distressed at *any* good fortune, while the spiteful man is so far from feeling distress that he actually rejoices.

However, we shall have occasion to continue this discussion elsewhere. After that we shall treat of justice, distinguishing its two kinds – because the word is used in more senses than one – and explain in what way each of them is a mean. [We shall also treat similarly of the rational virtues.]

VIII.
The mean is often nearer to one extreme than to the other, or seems nearer because of our natural tendencies

Thus there are three dispositions, two of them vicious (one by way of excess, the other of deficiency) and one good, the mean. They are all in some way opposed to one another: the extremes are contrary both to the mean and to each other, and the mean to the extremes. For just as the equal is greater compared with the less, and less compared with the greater, so the mean states (in both feelings and actions) are excessive compared with the deficient and deficient compared with the excessive. A brave man appears rash compared with a coward, and cowardly compared with a rash man; similarly a temperate man appears licentious compared with an insensible one and insensible compared with a licentious one, and a liberal man prodigal compared with an illiberal one and illiberal compared with a prodigal one. This is the reason why each extreme type tries to push the mean nearer to the other: the coward calls the brave man rash, the rash man calls him a coward; and similarly in all other cases. But while all these dispositions are opposed to one another in this way, the greatest degree of contrariety is that which is found between the two extremes. For they are separated by a greater interval from one another than from the mean, just as the great is further from the small, and the small from the great, than either is from the equal. Again, some extremes seem to bear a resemblance to a mean; e.g. rashness seems like courage, and prodigality like liberality; but between the extremes there is always the maximum dissimilarity. Now

45

contraries are by definition as far distant as possible from one
another; hence the further apart things are, the more contrary they will be. In some cases it is the deficiency, in others
the excess, that is more opposed to the mean; for instance,
the more direct opposite of courage is not the excess, rashness, but the deficiency, cowardice; and that of temperance
is not the deficiency, insensibility, but the excess, licentiousness. This result is due to two causes. One lies in the nature
of the thing itself. When one extreme has a closer affinity
and resemblance to the mean, we tend to oppose to the mean
not that extreme but the other. For instance, since rashness
is held to be nearer to courage and more like it than cowardice is, it is cowardice that we tend to oppose to courage,
because the extremes that are further from the mean are
thought to be more opposed to it. This is one cause, the one
that lies in the *thing*. The other lies in ourselves. It is the things
towards which we have the stronger natural inclination that
seem to us more opposed to the mean. For example, we are
naturally more inclined towards pleasures, and this makes
us more prone towards licentiousness than towards temperance; so we describe as more contrary to the mean those
things towards which we have the stronger tendency. This
is why licentiousness, the excess, is more contrary to
temperance.

IX.

Summing-up of the foregoing discussion, together with three practical rules for good conduct

We have now said enough to show that moral virtue is a
mean, and in what sense it is so: that it is a mean between
two vices, one of excess and the other of deficiency, and that

it is such because it aims at hitting the mean point in feelings and actions. For this reason it is a difficult business to be good; because in any given case it is difficult to find the mid-point – for instance, not everyone can find the centre of a circle; only the man who knows how. So too it is easy to get angry – anyone can do that – or to give and spend money; but to feel or act towards the right person to the right extent at the right time for the right reason in the right way – that is not easy, and it is not everyone that can do it. Hence to do these things well is a rare, laudable and fine achievement.

For this reason anyone who is aiming at the mean should (1) keep away from that extreme which is more contrary to the mean, just as Calypso advises: 'Far from this surf and surge keep thou thy ship.' For one of the extremes is always more erroneous than the other; and since it is extremely difficult to hit the mean, we must take the next best course, as they say, and choose the lesser of the evils; and this will be most readily done in the way that we are suggesting. (2) We must notice the errors into which we ourselves are liable to fall (because we all have different natural tendencies – we shall find out what ours are from the pleasure and pain that they give us), and we must drag ourselves in the contrary direction; for we shall arrive at the mean by pressing well away from our failing – just like somebody straightening a warped piece of wood. (3) In every situation one must guard especially against pleasure and pleasant things, because we are not impartial judges of pleasure. So we should adopt the same attitude towards it as the Trojan elders did towards Helen, and constantly repeat their pronouncement; because if in this way we relieve ourselves of the attraction, we shall be less likely to go wrong.

To sum up: by following these rules we shall have the best

chance of hitting the mean. But this is presumably difficult, especially in particular cases; because it is not easy to determine what is the right way to be angry, and with whom, and on what grounds, and for how long. Indeed we sometimes praise those who show deficiency, and call them patient, and sometimes those who display temper, calling them manly. However, the man who deviates only a little from the right degree, either in excess or in deficiency, is not censured – only the one who goes too far, because he is noticeable. Yet it is not easy to define by rule for how long, and how much, a man may go wrong before he incurs blame; no easier than it is to define any other object of perception. Such questions of degree occur in particular cases, and the decision lies with our perception.

This much, then, is clear: in all our conduct it is the mean that is to be commended. But one should incline sometimes towards excess and sometimes towards deficiency, because in this way we shall most easily hit upon the mean, that is, the right course.

III *Moral Responsibility: Two Virtues*

I.
Actions are voluntary, involuntary or non-voluntary

Since moral goodness is concerned with feelings and actions, and those that are voluntary receive praise and blame, whereas those that are involuntary receive pardon and sometimes pity too, students of moral goodness must presumably determine the limits of the voluntary and involuntary. Such a course is useful also for legislators with a view to prescribing honours and punishments.

Actions are regarded as involuntary when they are performed under compulsion or through ignorance. An act is compulsory when it has an external origin of such a kind that the agent or patient contributes nothing to it; e.g. if a voyager were to be conveyed somewhere by the wind or by men who had him in their power. But sometimes the act is done through fear of something worse, or for some admirable purpose; e.g. if a tyrant who has a man's parents and children in his power were to order him to do something dishonourable on condition that if he did it their lives would be spared, and if he did not they would be put to death: in these cases it is debatable whether the actions are involuntary or voluntary. A similar difficulty occurs with regard to jettisoning cargo in bad weather. In general no one willingly throws away his property; but if it is to save the lives of himself and everyone else, any reasonable person will do it. Such actions are mixed, although they seem more like voluntary than involuntary ones; because at the time that they are performed they are matters of choice, and the end of an action varies with the occasion; so the terms voluntary and involuntary should be used with reference to the time when the actions are performed. Now in cases like the above the agent acts voluntarily; because the movement of the limbs that are the instruments of action has its origin in the agent himself, and where this is so it is in his power either to act or not. Therefore such actions are voluntary; but considered absolutely they are presumably involuntary, because nobody would choose to do anything of this sort in itself. Sometimes people are actually praised for such actions, when they endure some disgrace or suffering as the price of great and splendid results; but if the case is the other way round, they are blamed, because to endure the utmost humiliation to serve no fine or even respectable end is the mark of a depraved nature. In some cases, however, the action, though not commended, is pardoned: namely, when a man acts wrongly because the alternative is too much for human nature, and nobody could endure it. But presumably there are some things such that a man cannot be compelled to do them – that he must sooner die than do, though he suffer the most dreadful fate. Indeed the reasons that 'compelled' Alcmaeon in Euripides' play to kill his mother seem absurd. Yet it is sometimes difficult to decide what sort of advantage is to be chosen at what sort of price, or what fate endured for the sake of what advantage; and it is still harder to abide by one's decisions. For the expected consequences are usually unpleasant, and what people are forced to do is discreditable; which is why agents are praised or blamed according to whether they have yielded to compulsion or not.

What sort of acts, then, ought we to call compulsory? Surely we should call them compulsory without qualification when the cause is external and the agent contributes nothing to it; whereas acts that are in themselves involuntary but are preferable at a given time and at a given cost, and that have their origin in the agent, although they are involuntary in themselves, nevertheless are voluntary at the given time and cost. They are more like voluntary acts, because actions belong to the sphere of particulars, and here the particular acts are voluntary. But what sort of acts are to be preferred, and to what alternatives and at what cost to the agent, is not an easy point to decide; because the differences in particular cases are many.

If it were argued that pleasurable and admirable things have a compulsive effect (because they bring external pressure to bear on us), it would make all acts compulsory; because every act of every agent is done for the sake of such objects. Also, to act under compulsion and against one's will is painful, but to act for a pleasurable or admirable object is pleasant. Also, it is absurd for the agent to lay the blame on external factors and not on himself for falling an easy prey to them, and to attribute his fine acts to himself but his disgraceful ones to the attractions of pleasure. It seems likely, then, that an act is compulsory only when its originating cause is external and receives no contribution from the person under compulsion.

Every act done through ignorance is non-voluntary, but it is involuntary only when it causes the agent subsequent pain and repentance. For if a man has done any act through ignorance and is not in the least upset about it, although he has not acted voluntarily (not knowing what he was doing), he has not acted involuntarily either, since he feels no pain.

Thus when a man repents of an act done through ignorance, he is considered to have acted involuntarily: but a man who does not repent of such an act is another case, so he may be said to have acted non-voluntarily; since he is different, it is better that he should have a name of his own.

Also, it seems that there is a distinction between acting *through* ignorance and acting *in* ignorance. When a man is drunk or in a rage his actions are considered to be the result not of ignorance but of one of the said conditions; but he acts not knowingly but *in* ignorance. As a matter of fact, every bad man is ignorant of what he ought to do and refrain from doing, and it is just this sort of fault that makes people unjust and generally bad. An act is not properly called involuntary if the agent is ignorant of his own advantage; for what makes an act involuntary is not ignorance in the choice (this is a cause of wickedness) nor ignorance of the universal (for this people are blamed), but *particular* ignorance, i.e. of the circumstances and objects of the action; for it is on these that pity and pardon depend, because a man who acts in ignorance of any such detail is an involuntary agent.

It will probably not be a bad thing, then, to determine the nature and number of these particular circumstances. They are (1) the agent, (2) the act, (3) the object or medium of the act, and sometimes also (4) the instrument (e.g. a tool), (5) the aim (e.g. saving life) and (6) the manner (e.g. gently or roughly). Now nobody in his right mind could be ignorant of *all* these circumstances. Obviously he cannot be ignorant of (I) the agent either – how can he fail to know himself? But he may not realize (2) what he is doing; as people say that they were 'carried away while speaking', or 'did not know it was a secret' (as in the case of Aeschylus and the Mysteries), or like the man who let off the catapult 'because he wanted to show how it worked'. Or (3) a person might actually think, like Merope, that his son was an enemy; or (4) that a sharp-pointed spear had a button on it, or that a stone was a piece of pumice, or (5) one might kill someone with a dose of a drug intended to save his life or (6) hit one's opponent when one meant only to seize his hand, as in finger wrestling. All these particular circumstances of an action admit of ignorance, and anyone who is ignorant of any of them is considered to have acted involuntarily, especially in the case of the most important of them, which are supposed to be the circumstances of the act and its effect. Further, for an act to be called involuntary in virtue of this sort of ignorance, the agent must also feel distress and repentance for having done it.

If an involuntary act is one performed under compulsion or as a result of ignorance, a voluntary act would seem to be one of which the originating cause lies in the agent himself, who knows the particular circumstances of his action. It is probably wrong to say that acts due to temper or desire are involuntary; for on this view in the first place the capacity for voluntary action will not extend to any animal other than man, or even to children; and secondly, when we act from desire or temper are none of our actions voluntary? Or are our fine actions done voluntarily and our discreditable ones involuntarily? Surely this is a ridiculous distinction, since the cause is one and the same; and it is presumably absurd to describe as involuntary acts to which we are rightly attracted. There are some things at which we actually ought to feel angry, and others that we actually ought to desire – health, for instance, and learning. Also what is involuntary is considered to be disagreeable, and what accords with our desire pleasant. Besides, what difference is there in point of voluntariness between wrong actions that are calculated and wrong actions that are due to temper? Both are to be avoided; and the irrational feelings are considered to be no less part of human nature than our considered judgements. It follows that actions due to temper or desire are also proper to the human agent. Therefore it is absurd to class these actions as involuntary.

II.
*Moral conduct implies choice, but what
is choice? It must be distinguished from
desire, temper, wish and opinion*

Now that we have determined the limits of the voluntary and the involuntary, our next task is to discuss choice; because it is felt to be very closely related to moral goodness, and to be a better test of character than actions are.

Now choice is clearly a voluntary thing, but the two words have not the same connotation: that of 'voluntary' is wider; for both children and animals have a share in voluntary action, but not in choice; and we call actions done on the spur of the moment voluntary, but not the result of choice.

Those who identify it with desire or temper or wish or some kind of opinion seem to do so mistakenly. Choice is not shared with man by irrational creatures as desire and temper are. Moreover, the incontinent man acts from desire but not from choice, while contrariwise the continent man acts from choice but not from desire. Again, a desire can be contrary to choice, but not to another desire. Again, desire is concerned with what is pleasurable and painful, but choice with neither. Still less is choice to be identified with temper; for acts due to temper are thought to involve choice less than any others. Nor, again, is choice wish, although it is obvious that there is a close connection between them. There is no choice of impossibilities, and anyone who professed to choose one would be thought silly; but one can wish for what is impossible, e.g. immortality. Also one can wish for results which one could not possibly bring about oneself, e.g. the success of a particular actor or athlete; but nobody *chooses* things like that – only what he thinks could be achieved by his own efforts. Again, wish is more concerned with the end, and choice with the means: e.g. we wish to be healthy, but choose things that will make us healthy; and we actually say 'we wish to be happy', but to say 'we choose to be happy' is incongruous, because in general choice seems to be concerned with acts that lie in our own power. Neither can it be opinion, for opinion seems to cover everything – things eternal or impossible no less than those that lie in our own power. Besides, opinions are distinguished by being true or false, not good or bad, which is rather the distinction between kinds of choice. Probably, then, no one even suggests that choice is the same as opinion in general; but neither is it the same as any particular opinion; for our characters are determined by our choice of what is good or evil, not by our opinion about it. Again, when we choose, it is to take or avoid something good or bad; but when we form an opinion, it is of what a thing is, or whom it benefits or how; but we do not really form an opinion of taking or avoiding. Again, a choice is more properly praised for choosing the right object than for being correct in itself; but an opinion is praised for being in accordance with the truth. Also we choose what we know very well to be good, but we form opinions about things that we do not really know to be good. It seems, too, that the same people are not equally good at choosing the best actions and forming the best opinions; some are comparatively good at forming opinions, but through a moral defect fail to make the right choices. Whether the forming of an opinion is prior to, or simultaneous with, an act of choice is immaterial; what we are investigating is not that, but whether choice is the same as a kind of opinion.

If, then, choice is none of the things that we have mentioned, what is it? what is its specific quality? Obviously what is chosen is voluntary, but not everything that is voluntary is chosen. Well, is it the result of previous deliberation? For choice implies a rational principle, and thought. The name, too, seems to indicate something that is chosen *before* other things.

III.
If choice involves deliberation, what
is the sphere of the latter?

Do people deliberate about all issues – i.e. is everything an object of deliberation? – or are there some things that do not admit of it? (Presumably we should call an object of deliberation what might be deliberated by a reasonable person, not by a fool or a madman.) Surely nobody deliberates about eternal facts, such as the order of the universe or the incommensurability of the diagonal with the side of a square; nor about eternal regular processes, whether they have a necessary or a natural or some other kind of cause – such as the solstices, or the risings of the sun; nor about irregular happenings like droughts and heavy rainstorms; nor about chance occurrences, like the finding of a treasure; for none of these results could be effected by our agency. What we deliberate about is practical measures that lie in our power; this is the class of things that actually remains, for the accepted types of cause are nature, necessity and chance, and also mind and human agency of all kinds. Not even all human affairs are objects of deliberation; thus no Spartan deliberates about the best form of constitution for the Scythians; each of the various groups of human beings deliberates about the practical measures that lie in its own power. Deliberation is not concerned with those branches of knowledge that have precise rules of their own (e.g. writing, for we do not hesitate over the way in which a word should be written). The effects about which we deliberate are those which are produced by our agency but not always in the same way; e.g. the practice of medicine and of finance, and of navigation – which calls for more deliberation than physical training does, inasmuch as it has not been reduced to such a precise system; and similarly also with the other occupations. The arts call for more deliberation than the sciences, because we feel less certain about them. Thus the field of deliberation is 'that which happens for the most part, where the result is obscure and the right course not clearly defined'; and for important decisions we call in advisers, distrusting our own ability to reach a decision.

Deliberation is about means, not ends

We deliberate not about ends but about means. A doctor does not deliberate whether to cure his patient, nor a speaker whether to persuade his audience, nor a statesman whether to produce law and order; nor does anyone else deliberate about the end at which he is aiming. They first set some end before themselves, and then proceed to consider how and by what means it can be attained. If it appears that it can be attained by several means, they further consider by which it can be attained best and most easily. If it can only be achieved by one means, they consider how it will be brought about by this, and then by what other means this will be brought about, until they arrive at the first cause, which is the last in the order of discovery (because the process of deliberation by the method described is like the investigation or analysis of a geometrical problem – it seems that not every investigation is a kind of deliberation, e.g. those of mathematics are not; but every deliberation is an investigation – and the last step in the analysis is the first in the process). If they then encounter an impossibility – e.g. if money is needed and cannot be provided – they give up; but if the thing appears possible, they set about doing it. By possible I mean those things that can be done by our agency (for the results of our friends' actions are in a sense results of our own, because the originating cause is in us). The question is sometimes what tools to use, and sometimes what use to make of them; similarly in other activities it is sometimes what means to use, and sometimes how to use it or how to secure it.

It seems, then, as we have said, that the originating cause of actions is a man, and the field of deliberation is what is practicable for the agent; and that the actions are for the sake of something else. The object of deliberation, then, cannot be the end, but must be the means to ends. Nor again is deliberation concerned with particular facts, such as 'is it a loaf?' or 'is it properly cooked?'; these are matters for sense-perception. And if one is to deliberate in every case, the process will go on to infinity.

The object of deliberation and the object of choice are the same, except that the latter has already been determined; it has been selected as the result of deliberation. In every case a man stops inquiring how to act when he has traced the starting-point of action back to himself, i.e. to the dominant part of himself; for it is this that makes the choice. This is evident also from the ancient constitutions as portrayed by Homer – the kings proclaimed to the people what they had already chosen to do.

Definition of choice

Since, therefore, an object of choice is something within our power at which we aim after deliberation, choice will be a deliberate appetition of things that lie in our power. For we first make a decision as the result of deliberation, and then direct our aim in accordance with the deliberation.

This may serve as an outline account of choice, and the sort of objects with which it is concerned, and the fact that it is a choice of means towards an end.

IV.
The object of wish is in one sense the good, in another the apparent good

We have already said that wish is concerned with the end; but some think that its object is the good, and others that it is the *apparent* good. Now for those who hold that the object of wish is the good it follows that if a person chooses wrongly, what he wishes is not an object of wish (because if it is wishable it must be good; but it may in fact have been bad); while on the other hand for those who hold that what is wished is the *apparent* good it follows that nothing is by nature wishable, but that what any individual thinks is good is wishable for him – and different people have different and, it may be, contrary views.

If these consequences are unacceptable, perhaps we should say that absolutely and in truth the object of wish is the good, but for the individual it is what seems good to him; so for the man of good character it is the true good, but for the bad man it is any chance thing. It is just the same as it is with physical conditions. What is wholesome for those who are in good health is what is really wholesome; but what is wholesome for invalids is something different (and similarly with things bitter and sweet, hot and heavy, and every other kind of object). For the man of good character judges every situation rightly; i.e. in every situation what appears to him is the truth. Every disposition has its own appreciation of what is fine and pleasant; and probably what makes the man of good character stand out furthest is the fact that he sees the truth in every kind of situation: he is a sort of standard and yardstick of what is fine and pleasant. Most people seem to owe their deception to pleasure, which appears to them to be a good although it is not; consequently they choose what is pleasant as a good, and avoid pain as an evil.

v.

Actions that we initiate ourselves, whether they are good or bad, are voluntary

Since, while the end is an object of wish, the means to it are objects of deliberation and choice, the actions that are related to the means will be performed in accordance with choice, and voluntarily. But the exercise of moral virtues is related to means. Therefore virtue lies in our power, and similarly so does vice; because where it is in our power to act, it is also in our power not to act, and where we can refuse we can also comply. So if it is in our power to do a thing when it is right, it will also be in our power not to do it when it is wrong; and if it is in our power not to do it when it is right, it will also be in our power to do it when it is wrong. And if it is in our power to do right and wrong, and similarly not to do them; and if, as we saw, doing right or wrong is the essence of being good or bad, it follows that it is in our power to be decent or worthless. The saying, 'None would be evil, or would not be blessed', seems to be partly false and partly true; because nobody is unwilling to be blessed, but wickedness is voluntary. Otherwise we must dispute what we have just been saying, and assert that man is *not* the originator or begetter of his own actions as he is of his children. But if it is manifestly true that he *is*, and we cannot refer our actions to any other sources than those that are in ourselves, then the actions whose sources are in us are themselves in our power, i.e. voluntary.

This is borne out by the common use of rewards and punishments

This view seems to be supported by the practice both of the various groups privately and of the legislators themselves; for they impose punishments and penalties upon malefactors (except where the offence is committed under duress or in unavoidable ignorance), and bestow honours on those who do fine actions; which implies that their object is to encourage the latter and restrain the former. But nobody is encouraged to do an act which is neither in our power nor voluntary; it is assumed that there is no point in our being persuaded not to get hot or feel pain or hunger or anything else of that sort, because we shall feel them just the same.

Responsibility for the results of bad moral states

Indeed they punish the offender for his very ignorance, if he is thought to be responsible for it. E.g. penalties are doubled for committing an offence in a state of drunkenness, because the source of the action lay in the agent himself: he was capable of not getting drunk, and his drunkenness was the cause of his ignorance. They also punish ignorance of any point of law that ought to be known and is not difficult to ascertain. Similarly too in all other cases where the offenders' ignorance is considered to be due to negligence, on the ground that it was in their power not to be ignorant, because they were capable of taking care.

'Well, probably he is the sort of person that doesn't take care.' But people get into this condition through their own fault, by the slackness of their lives; i.e. they make themselves unjust or licentious by behaving dishonestly or spending their time in drinking and other forms of dissipation; for in every sphere of conduct people develop qualities corresponding to the activities that they pursue. This is evident from the example of people training for any competition or undertaking: they spend all their time in exercising. So to be unaware that in every department of conduct moral states are the result of corresponding activities is the mark of a thoroughly unperceptive person.

A bad moral state, once formed, is not easily amended

Again, it is unreasonable to suppose that a man who acts unjustly or licentiously does not wish to be unjust or licentious; and if anyone, without being in ignorance, acts in a way that will make him unjust, he will be voluntarily unjust; but it does not follow that he can stop being unjust, and be just, if he wants to – no more than a sick man can become healthy, even though (it may be) his sickness is voluntary, being the result of incontinent living and disobeying his doctors. There was a time when it was open to him not to be ill; but when he had once thrown away his chance, it was gone; just as when one has once let go of a stone, it is too late to get it back – but the agent was responsible for throwing it, because the origin of the action was in himself. So too it was at first open to the unjust and licentious persons not to become such, and therefore they are voluntarily what they are; but now that they have become what they are, it is no longer open to them not to be such.

Even physical defects, if voluntarily incurred, are culpable

It is not only vices of the soul that are voluntary; physical defects too are voluntarily incurred by some people, and we blame them for it. Nobody blames those who are naturally ugly, but we do blame those who become so through lack of exercise and care for their appearance. Similarly too in the case of physical weakness and disability. Nobody would criticize a person who is blind by nature or as a result of disease or injury – he would more likely be an object of pity – but anyone would blame a person whose blindness is due to heavy drinking or some other self-indulgence. Thus physical defects for which we are responsible are blamed, but those for which we are not responsible are not blamed. And if this is so, then in the case of moral defects too those that are blamed will be ones for which we are responsible.

It may be objected that moral discernment is a gift of nature and cannot be acquired otherwise

But suppose that somebody says, 'Everyone aims at what appears to him to be good, but over this appearance people have no control. How the end appears to each individual depends on the nature of his character, whatever this may be. Then if the individual is in a manner responsible for his moral state, he will also be in a manner himself responsible for his view of what is good; but if he is *not* responsible for the former, then no wrongdoer is responsible for doing wrong; he does it through ignorance of the end, because he thinks that by this conduct he will achieve what is best for him. His aiming at the end is not a matter of his choosing; he must be born with it as a sort of vision to enable him to judge correctly and choose what is truly good. A man of good natural disposition is one who is well endowed in this way, for he will possess as a natural gift the finest and most important thing in the world, which cannot be had or learnt from another; and to be well and rightly endowed in this respect will be to have true and perfect goodness of disposition.'

Even so, virtue will be no more voluntary than vice

Now if this is a true statement of the facts, how will virtue be more voluntary than vice? The end is envisaged and decided upon in the same way – whether through natural ability or otherwise – by both good and bad; and it is with reference to this end that they perform all their other actions, of whatever kind. So whether (1) the individual's view of the end – whatever it may be – is *not* supplied by nature, but depends partly on himself, or (2) the end *is* the gift of nature, but virtue is voluntary because the good man performs voluntarily all the means towards the end – in either case vice will be no less voluntary; because the bad man has just as much independence in his *actions*, even if not in his choice of the end. So if, as is asserted, our virtues are voluntary (because we ourselves are in a sense partly responsible for our dispositions, and it is because we have a certain moral quality that we assume the end to be of a certain kind), our vices will be voluntary too; the cases are similar.

We have now given a general account of the virtues, stating in outline what their genus is, namely that they are mean states and dispositions; and that they of themselves enable their possessor to perform the same sort of actions as those by which they are acquired; and that they are under our control and are voluntary; and act as the right principle prescribes. But our dispositions are not voluntary in the same sense that our actions are. Our actions are under our control from beginning to end, because we are aware of the individual stages, but we only control the beginning of our dispositions; the individual stages of their development, as in the case of illness, are unnoticeable. They are, however, voluntary in the sense that it was originally in our power to exercise them in one way or the other.

Now to discuss the virtues one by one

Let us now resume our discussion of the virtues, taking them one by one, and explaining what each is, and with what sort of objects it is concerned and in what way. At the same time it will become clear how many virtues there are.

VI.

Courage: the right attitude towards feelings of fear and confidence. What we ought and ought not to fear

Let us begin with courage. It has already been shown that it is a mean state in relation to feelings of fear and confidence. Obviously the things that we fear are fearful, and such things are, broadly speaking, evils; which is why some people define fear as an expectation of evil. Well, we do fear all evils – e.g. disgrace, poverty, sickness, friendlessness, death – but not all of these are considered to be the concern of the courageous man, because there are some of them that it is right and honourable to fear, and shameful not to fear, e.g. disgrace. The man who is afraid of it is upright and decent, and the man who is not afraid of it is shameless; but he is sometimes called courageous by a transference of meaning, because he has a point of similarity to a courageous man: the latter is also a sort of fearless person.

Probably one ought not to fear poverty or disease, nor in general anything that is not the result of vice or one's own fault; but a person who feels no fear about these things is not courageous either (although he too is called so by analogy), because some people who are cowardly in the perils of war are liberal with their money and face the loss of it with equanimity. And surely a man is not a coward if he dreads brutality towards his wife and children, or envy or anything of this kind; nor is he brave if he is undismayed at the prospect of a flogging.

What, then, are the terrors with which the courageous man is concerned? Surely the greatest, because nobody is better able to endure dreadful experiences. Now the most fearful thing of all is death; for it is the end, and it is assumed that for the dead there is no good or evil any more. But it may be thought that even death does not in all its forms afford scope for courage; e.g. death at sea, or in illness. Death in what circumstances, then? Surely in the noblest; and this describes deaths in warfare, where the danger is greatest and most glorious. This is borne out by the honours paid to the fallen both in city-states and at the courts of monarchs. So in the strict sense of the word the courageous man will be one who is fearless in the face of an honourable death, or of some sudden threat of death; and it is in war that such situations chiefly occur. Of course the courageous man will be fearless on the sea too (or in outbreaks of disease); but not in the same way as a seaman is, because the landsmen have given up all hope of being saved and are revolted by the thought of such a death, but the seamen have high hopes because of their experience. Also, courage can be shown in situations that give scope for stout resistance or a glorious death; but in a disaster of this kind there is no place for either.

VII.
Degrees of fear and fearfulness

What is terrible is not the same for all persons. There is a kind of thing that we describe as beyond human endurance, and this is fearful to any reasonable person; but things within the limits of human endurance differ in the magnitude and intensity of the fear that they inspire (and similarly with things that inspire confidence). The courageous man, however, is undaunted, so far as is humanly possible; he will fear what it is natural for man to fear, but he will face it in the right way and as principle directs, for the sake of what is right and honourable; for this is the end of virtue. But it is possible to fear these things too much or too little, and also to fear what is not fearful as if it were. One kind of error is to be afraid of the wrong thing, another to be afraid in the wrong way, and another at the wrong time or with some other such qualification (and similarly with things that inspire confidence). The man who faces and fears (or similarly feels confident about) the right things for the right reason and in the right way and at the right time is courageous (for the courageous man feels and acts duly, and as principle directs); and the end of every activity is that which accords with the disposition corresponding to that activity. This is true of the courageous man. His courage is a noble thing, so its end is of the same kind, because the nature of any given thing is determined by its end. Thus it is for a right and noble motive that the courageous man faces the dangers and performs the actions appropriate to his courage.

Excessive fearlessness, rashness and cowardice

The person who carries fearlessness too far has no distinctive name (we have noted above that many types are nameless), but if he were afraid of nothing – not even of an earthquake or inundation, as they say of the Celts – he would be a maniac or insensate. The man who exceeds in confidence about things that are fearful is rash. The rash man is considered to be both a boaster and a pretender to courage; at any rate he wishes to *seem* as the courageous man really *is* in his attitude towards fearful situations, and therefore imitates him where he can. Hence such people are usually cowardly as well as rash, because while they make a show of confidence when circumstances permit, they cannot face anything fearful.

The man who exceeds in fearing is a coward. He fears the wrong things and in the wrong way, and all the other similar qualifications attach to him. He also shows a deficiency in confidence; but he is more easily identified by his excessive reaction in cases of pain. Thus the coward is a despondent sort of person, because he is afraid of everything; whereas the courageous man is in the opposite case, because confidence is the mark of optimism.

Thus the coward, the rash man and the courageous man are all concerned with the same things, but differ in their attitudes towards them. The two former show excess and deficiency, but the other has the right disposition and observes the mean. Rash people are impetuous, eager before danger arrives but shifty when it is actually present; whereas courageous ones are keen at the time of action but calm beforehand.

So, as we have said, courage is a mean state in relation to things conducive to confidence or fear in the circumstances described; it feels confidence or faces danger because this is a fine thing to do, or it is a disgrace not to do it. But to kill oneself to escape from poverty or love or anything else that is distressing is not courageous but rather the act of a coward, because it shows weakness of character to run away from hardships, and the suicide endures death not because it is a fine thing to do but in order to escape from suffering.

VIII.
Five dispositions that resemble courage

(1) Civic courage

Such, then, is the nature of courage; but the name is also applied to five other kinds of behaviour under five heads.

Civic courage comes first because it is very like courage proper; for citizens are considered to face their dangers not only because of the legal penalties and the disgrace, but also because of the honours. This is why those peoples are thought bravest among whom cowards are despised and brave men held in honour. Homer represents such characters, e.g. Diomede and Hector:

Polydamas will be the first to cast reproach at me;

and Diomede says:

For one day Hector will proclaim among the host
   of Troy
'The son of Tydeus by my hand . . .'

This courage has the closest resemblance of all to courage as described above, because its ground is a moral virtue: a proper sense of shame, and a desire for something noble (that is, honour) and avoidance of reproach, which is a disgrace. And one might place in the same rank those who are compelled to face death by their commanders; but they are inferior inasmuch as they do so not through shame but through fear, and what they shun is not dishonour but pain. Their officers compel them as Hector does:

That man of you that I shall mark skulking behind
   the lines –
He shall not save his carcase from the dogs . . .

The same policy is followed by those who line their men up in front of them and beat them if they give ground, and those who post their men in front of trenches and other such obstacles – they are all using compulsion. But one ought to be brave not under compulsion but because it is a fine thing.

(2) *Experience of risk*

Experience of particular kinds of risk is regarded as a form of courage (this is why Socrates thought that courage is a kind of knowledge). This sort of courage is shown by different types of person in different kinds of danger, but in the dangers of war it is shown by soldiers. It is accepted that there are many false alarms in war, of which these men are very well aware from their own observation; and so they appear to be brave, because other people do not know how groundless the alarms are. Then their experience makes them highly proficient in causing damage without suffering it, because they can use their weapons, and they carry the sort of arms that will be most effective both for attack and for defence. So they are like armed men fighting against the unarmed, and trained athletes against ordinary people; because in contests of this kind the best fighters are not the bravest men, but those who are strongest and fittest physically. On the other hand when the danger is extreme and they are inferior in numbers and equipment it is the professional soldiers that turn coward; they are the first to flee, while the citizen troops die at their posts – as happened in the fighting at the temple of Hermes. This is because to the latter running away is a disgrace, and death is preferable to saving their lives in such a way; but the others originally accepted the risk in the belief that they had the advantage, and when they find out their mistake they flee, because they fear death more than dishonour. But the courageous man is not like that.

(3) *Spirit or mettle*

Spirit is also referred to as courage, for those who act with spirit, like beasts charging those who have wounded them, are also considered to be courageous, because the courageous too are spirited (for spirit is very bold in the face of danger): hence Homer's phrases 'into their spirit he put strength' and 'rage he aroused and spirit' and 'bitter rage about his nostrils' and 'up boiled his blood'; for all these seem to indicate the rousing and impulse of the spirit. Courageous people act for a fine motive, and their spirit is an accessory; but beasts act under the influence of pain: it is because they have been injured or frightened; this is shown by the fact that in a forest they do not attack. Thus it does not mean that beasts are courageous simply because, impelled by pain and anger, they rush into danger, blind to the risks they run; if this were so, even donkeys would be brave when they are hungry, because they refuse to stop grazing even if you beat them. (Adulterers, too, are led on by their lust to do many reckless things.) The quasi-courage that is due to spirit seems to be the most natural, and if it includes deliberate choice and purpose it is considered to be courage. Human beings, too, feel pain when they get angry and pleasure when they retaliate; but those who fight for these reasons, although they may be good fighters, are not courageous, because they are acting not from a fine motive, nor on principle, but from feeling. Still, they bear a close resemblance to the courageous.

(4) Sanguineness or optimism

Nor, indeed, are sanguine people courageous. It is because they have often defeated many enemies that they are confident in danger. They are very similar to the courageous in that both are confident; but whereas the courageous are confident for the reasons stated above, the sanguine are confident because they think they are the best soldiers and cannot lose (this is how people behave when they get drunk: they become sanguine); but when the result does not turn out as expected, they run away. But as we saw, it is the mark of a courageous man to face things that are terrible to a human being, and that he can see are such, because it is a fine act to face them and a disgrace not to do so. This is why it is thought to be a better proof of courage to remain calm and undismayed in sudden alarms than in those that are foreseen: the action proceeds more directly from the moral state, because it is less the result of preparation. One may choose to face a foreseeable danger after calculation and reflection, but one faces sudden dangers only in virtue of the formed state of character.

(5) Ignorance

Those who act in ignorance, too, appear to be courageous. They are not far different from the sanguine, but they are inferior inasmuch as they have no self-confidence such as the sanguine have. Hence while the sanguine stand firm for a time, those who are under a misapprehension, if they find out or suspect that the situation is different from what they supposed, run away. This is just what happened to the Argives when they fell in with the Spartans under the impression that they were Sicyonians.

We have now described the different kinds of courage and supposed courage.

IX.
Courage in relation to pleasure and pain

Courage is concerned with grounds for confidence and fear, but not to the same degree with both; it is more concerned with what is fearful, because the man who is composed in the thick of dangers and meets them in the right spirit is more truly courageous than the one who behaves similarly in encouraging circumstances. Indeed, as we have said, people are called courageous for enduring pain. Hence courage implies the presence of pain, and it is rightly praised, because it is harder to bear pain than to abstain from pleasure. It may, of course, be thought that the *end* of an act which involves courage is pleasant, but that this fact is obscured by the attendant circumstances, just as happens in athletic contests. The end or purpose of the boxers, i.e. the wreath and the honours, is pleasant; but it hurts to take punches if you are made of flesh and blood – it is painful, and so is all their laborious training. And because these hardships are so many, their object, being small by comparison, seems to entail no pleasure. Now if it is like this in the case of courage, death and wounds will be painful to the courageous man, and he will not willingly endure them; but endure them he will, because that is the fine thing to do, or because it is a disgrace not to endure them. And the more completely a man possesses virtue, and the happier he is, the more he will be distressed at the thought of death. For to such a man life is supremely worth living; and he is losing the greatest blessings, and he knows it; and this is a grievous thing. But that does not make him any less brave; he is probably even braver for it, because in preference to these blessings he chooses a gallant end in war. It is not true, then, of every virtue that the exercise of it is pleasurable, except in so far as one attains the end. Presumably it is quite possible that the best professional soldiers are made not out of men like this but of others who are less brave but have nothing apart from their lives to lose; because the latter are ready to meet dangers, and sell their lives for petty gains.

So much for our account of courage. In the light of what has been said it should not be difficult to grasp (in outline at any rate) what courage is.

x.
Temperance or self-control, and the pleasures with which it is concerned

Next after courage let us say something about temperance, because these two virtues are considered to belong to the irrational parts of the soul. We have already said that temperance is a mean state with regard to pleasures (for it is less concerned with pains, and in a different way). Licentiousness is shown in the same field. So let us now determine with what kind of pleasures they are concerned.

Pleasures are either psychical or physical

We must first distinguish pleasures of the soul from pleasures of the body. Examples of the former are love of civic distinction and love of learning. In either case when the subject enjoys what he loves it is not his body that is affected but rather his mind; and those who are concerned with pleasures of this sort are called neither temperate nor licentious. Similarly with all others who are concerned with pleasures that are not physical. Those who like to hear marvellous tales or to relate anecdotes or to spend their days in aimless gossip we call idle and talkative, but not licentious; nor should we so describe those who are grieved at the loss of money or friends.

It is the pleasures of the body, then, that are the concern of temperance; but not even all of them. Those who enjoy the objects of sight, like colours and shapes and pictures, are called neither temperate nor licentious. It may be supposed, however, that even in the case of these pleasure can be felt in the right degree, or too much, or too little. Similarly with the objects of hearing. Nobody calls people licentious for taking an inordinate pleasure in listening to music or an actor's voice, nor temperate if their enjoyment was duly restrained. Nor do we speak in this way about those who enjoy smells, except those who do so by association. We do not call those who enjoy the smell of apples or roses or incense licentious; we apply this description rather to those who enjoy the smell of perfume and savoury dishes, for these are what licentious people enjoy, because through them they are reminded of the objects of their desires. One can see that others too enjoy the smell of food when they are hungry; but the enjoyment of such things is characteristic of the licentious person, because to him they are objects of desire. Animals do not experience pleasure through their senses, either, except by association; it is not the smell of hares that hounds enjoy, but the eating of them; and the smell calls attention to their presence. Nor is it the lowing of an ox that a lion enjoys, but the feeding on it. The reason why he seems to enjoy the lowing is that it was through it that he became aware that the ox was near. Similarly he does not take pleasure in the sight of 'a deer or a wild goat', but in the fact that he is going to have a meal.

The grossest pleasures are those of
taste and, above all, touch

Thus temperance and licentiousness are concerned with such pleasures as are shared by animals too (which makes them regarded as low and brutish). These are touch and taste. But even taste seems to play a small part, if any. The function of taste is to distinguish flavours, as wine-tasters do, or cooks who are seasoning dishes. But it is not exactly the flavours that gratify, at least not the licentious person; it is rather the enjoyment, which depends entirely upon touch, whether in the case of food or of drink or of what is called sex. This is why one gourmet prayed that his throat might become longer than a crane's; which shows that he took pleasure in the actual contact.

Thus the sense that gives scope to licentiousness is the one that is most widely shared; and it would seem to be justly liable to reproach, because it attaches to us not as men but as animals. So to enjoy such sensations and find the greatest satisfaction in them is brutish. The most refined pleasures of touch are excepted – I mean those that are experienced at sports centres through the means of heat and massage – because for the licentious person touch is concerned only with certain parts of the body, not with the whole.

XI.
Desires or appetites; self-indulgence and insensibility

Desires seem to be either general or particular and adventitious. For example, the desire for food is natural, since everyone who needs food desires it either in solid or in liquid form, and sometimes in both; and similarly with sexual intercourse when, in Homer's phrase, he is young and lusty. But not everyone desires this or that particular kind of food or sex, or the same kind always; so that appetite seems to be a matter of personal taste. Nevertheless there is a natural element in it, because different things please different kinds of people, and some kinds are more than averagely pleasing to everyone.

Now in the case of natural desires few people go wrong, and only in one way, in the direction of too much; because to eat or drink indiscriminately until one is full to bursting is to exceed in quantity one's natural limit, since the natural desire is merely a replenishment of the deficiency. (Hence such people are called 'belly-mad', because they fill their bellies more than they ought. Those who behave in this way are extremely crude types of humanity.) But with regard to particular pleasures many people go wrong in many ways. Some of those who are called 'lovers' of this or that go wrong in enjoying the wrong objects, others in enjoying things with abnormal intensity, or in the wrong way; and the licentious display excess in every form. They enjoy some things that it is wrong to enjoy, because they are odious; and where it is right to enjoy something, they enjoy it more than is right, or more than is normal.

Clearly, then, excess in respect of pleasures is licentiousness, and a culpable thing. As for pains, the situation is not as it was in the case of courage: a person is not called temperate for enduring them and licentious for not doing so; the licentious man is so called for being unduly distressed at missing what is pleasant (thus even his pain is caused by pleasure), whereas the temperate man is so called for not being distressed by the absence of what is pleasant, or by abstinence from it. Thus the licentious man desires all pleasant things, or the most pleasant; and he is so carried away by his desire that he chooses them before anything else. Hence he feels pain both when he fails to get them and when he desires them (because desire involves pain); and it seems preposterous to feel pain on account of pleasure.

Cases of deficiency in respect of pleasures, that is of enjoying them less than one ought, hardly occur; because such insensibility is subhuman. Even the lower animals discriminate between different foods, and enjoy some but not others. If there is any creature to whom nothing is pleasant and everything indifferent, he must be very far from being human; and because such a type hardly occurs, it has not secured itself a name.

The temperate man holds a mean position with regard to pleasures. He enjoys neither the things that the licentious man enjoys most (he positively objects to them) nor wrong pleasures in general, nor does he enjoy any pleasure violently; he is not distressed by the absence of pleasures, nor does he desire them – or if he does, he desires them moderately, and not more than is right or at the wrong time or in general with any other such qualification. But such pleasures as conduce to health and bodily fitness he will try to secure in moderation and in the right way; and also all other pleasures that are not incompatible with these, or dishonourable or beyond his means. For the man who disregards these limitations sets too high a value on such pleasures; but the temperate man is not like that: he appreciates them as the right principle directs.

XII.

Licentiousness is more voluntary than cowardice

Licentiousness is more like a voluntary thing than cowardice. The former is caused by pleasure and the latter by pain, of which the one is to be chosen and the other avoided; and pain distracts the sufferer and impairs his natural state, but pleasure has no such effect; therefore licentiousness is more voluntary. Hence it is also more reprehensible, since it is easier to train oneself to resist pleasures, because there are plenty of such opportunities in life, and the methods of habituation involve no danger; but with terrors the reverse is the case. It might seem that cowardice is not voluntary in the same way that particular instances of cowardice are, because *it* involves no pain, but *they* so distract a person with pain that he even throws away his weapons and disgraces himself in every other way; and for this reason they are considered to be compulsive. But for the licentious man, on the contrary, particular acts are voluntary, since he does them from desire and appetite; but the condition as a whole is less so, because nobody *desires* to be licentious.

Licentious people are like spoilt children

We apply the name of licentiousness to the faults of children too, because they bear a certain resemblance to it. Which is called after the other makes no difference for our present purpose, but obviously the later use must come from the earlier. The metaphor seems not to be a bad one, because restraint is necessary for anything that has low appetites and a marked capacity for growth; and these qualities are possessed in the highest degree by desires and also by children. For children too live as their desires impel them, and it is in them that the appetite for pleasant things is strongest; so unless this is rendered docile and submissive to authority it will pass all bounds. For in an irrational being the appetite for what gives it pleasure is insatiable and indiscriminate, and the exercise of the desire increases its innate tendency; and if these appetites are strong and violent, they actually drive out reason. So they must be moderate and few, and in no way opposed to the dictates of principle – this is what we mean by 'docile' and 'restrained' – and just as the child ought to live in accordance with the directions of his tutor, so the desiderative element in us ought to be controlled by rational principle. Thus the desiderative element of the temperate man ought to be in harmony with the rational principle; because both have the same object: the attainment of what is admirable. Also the temperate man desires the right things in the right way and at the right time, and this also is pre-scribed by rational principle.

So much for our account of temperance.

x *Pleasure and the Life of Happiness*

I.

The importance of pleasure in ethics, and the conflict of views about its value

After this our next task is presumably to discuss pleasure; for it is generally agreed that pleasure is very closely bound up with human nature; which is why those who are educating the young keep them straight by the use of pleasure and pain. It is also thought to be most important for the forming of a virtuous character to like and dislike the right things; because pleasure and pain permeate the whole of life, and have a powerful influence upon virtue and the happy life, since people choose what is pleasant and avoid what is painful. It would seem most improper, then, to neglect such important factors, especially since they admit of a great deal of controversy.

One school maintains that pleasure is the good; another, on the contrary, that it is wholly bad: some of its members very likely from a conviction that it is really so, and others believing that it is better with a view to the conduct of our lives to represent pleasure as a bad thing, even if it is not; because (they say) most people are inclined towards it and are the slaves of their self-indulgence, so that they need to be urged in the opposite direction; for in this way they may attain to the mean. But probably this view is not correct. For in matters relating to feelings and actions theories are less reliable than facts; so when they clash with the evidence of our senses they provoke contempt and damage the cause of truth as well as their own. For if a person who denounces pleasure is ever observed to be drawn towards it himself, his backsliding is assumed to imply that he regards all pleasure as desirable; because most people are incapable of drawing distinctions. So it seems that true theories are extremely valuable for the conduct of our lives as well as for the acquisition of knowledge, since because of their agreement with the facts they carry conviction, and so encourage those who understand them to live under their direction.

But enough of these observations; let us examine the views that have been propounded about pleasure.

II.
Eudoxus' view, that pleasure is the supreme good, is not above dispute

Eudoxus thought that pleasure is the good, because he observed that all creatures, both rational and irrational, are attracted by it; and that in every case what is desirable is good, and what is most desirable is best; so the fact that all creatures are drawn in the same direction shows that this is what is best for all (since each individual tries to find its own good, just as it does its own food); and that which is good for all, and which all try to obtain, is the good. His arguments were accepted more for the excellence of his character than on their own account, because he was regarded as exceptionally self-controlled; so it was concluded that he did not state this view because he was a pleasure-lover, but that the facts really were so.

He thought that it was no less evident from consideration of its contrary, because pain, he thought, is in itself something to be shunned by all, and therefore similarly its contrary is to be chosen. He held also that the most desirable thing is that which we choose neither as a means to, nor for the sake of, something else; and that pleasure is, by common consent, a thing of this kind; for no one ever asks a man *why* he is enjoying himself, because it is assumed that pleasure is desirable in itself. He also said that the addition of pleasure to any good thing – e.g. just or temperate conduct – makes it more desirable; but what is good is only increased by itself. Now this particular argument seems only to show that pleasure is *a* good, no more good than any other; because any good thing is more desirable when accompanied by another than it is by itself. In fact Plato uses this sort of argument to refute the view that pleasure is the good; for he says that the life of pleasure is more desirable with the addition of intelligence than without it; and if the combination is better, pleasure is not the good; because no addition of anything else to the good makes it more desirable. And clearly nothing else can be the good either, if it becomes more desirable when accompanied by something that is good in itself. What, then, is there that cannot be made better by the addition of some good, and yet is something in which we share? because it is something of this sort that is the object of our inquiry.

III.

The view that pleasure is not a good is also open to criticism

On the other hand those who contend that what all creatures try to obtain is not a good are surely talking nonsense; for we hold that what everyone believes is so; and the man who tries to destroy this belief is not likely to have a more convincing account of his own. If it were only irrational creatures that are attracted by pleasure, there might be something in the theory; but if intelligent beings are attracted too, how can it be taken seriously? Presumably there is even in the lower animals some instinct superior to their own natures which tries to attain their proper good.

It does not seem that their argument about the contrary is valid either. They say that if pain is an evil, it does not follow that pleasure is a good, because an evil can be opposed to an evil, and both opposed to something that is neither good nor evil. There is nothing wrong with the argument, but it does not truly apply to the case under discussion. For if both pleasure and pain are evils, both should be objects of aversion; and if they are neutral, neither should be, or both should be equally, objects of aversion; but as it is we can see that people avoid the one as an evil and choose the other as a good. Therefore it is as good and evil that they are opposed.

Again, even if pleasure is not a quality, it does not follow that it is not a good; because good activities are not qualities either, nor is happiness.

They say that the good is determinate, whereas pleasure is indeterminate, because it admits of differences of degree. Now if they base this judgement on the fact that people are pleased in different degrees, the same argument will apply to justice and all the other virtues in respect of which people are said explicitly to possess qualities, and act in accordance with the virtues, in a greater or lesser degree; because one person is more just, or more brave, than another, and acts more justly or temperately than another. But if they are judging by the *pleasures*, it looks as if they are not stating the right ground for their conclusion, if pleasures are of two kinds, pure and mixed.

But why should not pleasure be determinate, just as health is, although it admits of degrees? For health does not consist of the same proportion in everyone; it is not even always one and the same in the same person, but when it is in process of breaking up it still persists up to a point, i.e. it exhibits differences of degree. So this explanation may fit the case of pleasure too.

They assume that the good is something perfect, whereas movements and processes are incomplete; and they try to show that pleasure is a movement or process. But their argument does not seem to be correct, and pleasure does not seem to be a movement. For it is accepted that every movement has its own quickness and slowness, relative if not to itself – as the movement of the universe is not – then relatively to something else. But neither alternative applies to pleasure. One can *become* pleased quickly, just as one can get angry, but not *be* pleased, not even in comparison with someone else, as one can walk or grow, etc. Thus it is possible to pass into a state of pleasure quickly or slowly, but not to actualize that state (i.e. be pleased) quickly. Again, how can pleasure be a process of becoming? It is accepted that development is not from *any* one thing into *any* other thing, but that everything is resolved into that from which it came; and where pleasure is the generation of something, pain is the destruction of that something. They also say that pain is a deficiency of our natural condition, and that pleasure is its replenishment. But these are *bodily* experiences. So if pleasure is a replenishment of the natural state, what will feel pleasure is that in which the replenishment takes place; so it will be the body that does so. But this is not generally accepted. So pleasure is not a process of replenishment, although the person in whom the process is going on may feel pleasure, as he would feel pain if he were being cut. This theory seems to have been derived from the pains and pleasures connected with eating: it is assumed that it is because we have experienced a lack, and felt pain, that we subsequently find pleasure in replenishment. But this does not happen in the case of all pleasures. The pleasures of learning, for instance, have no antecedent pains; neither have some even of the sensuous pleasures, such as those of smell, and many sounds and sights too, and memories and hopes. Of what, then, will these be generative processes? because no deficiency of anything has arisen that can be replenished.

Even the view that some pleasures are bad can be challenged

Against those who cite instances of disreputable pleasures one may argue that these pleasures are not pleasant. They may be pleasant to persons of an unhealthy disposition, but that does not compel us to believe that they are really pleasant (except to these persons), any more than that things are really wholesome or sweet or bitter that seem so to sick people, or that things are white that appear so to people with diseased eyes. Or one might argue that the pleasures are desirable in themselves, but not when they are achieved in a certain way; as, e.g., wealth is desirable, but not as the price of treason, and health is desirable, but not if it involves indiscriminate eating. Or that pleasures differ in kind; for those that come from noble acts are different from those that come from base ones, and it is impossible to enjoy the pleasure of a just man unless one is just, or that of a musical man unless one is musical, and so on. The difference between a flatterer and a friend seems to show that pleasure is not a good, or else that pleasures are different in kind; for the one is considered to associate with others for their good, and the other for their pleasure; and the fact that the latter is blamed whereas the former is praised implies that the objects of their companionship are different. Nobody would choose to live out his life with the mentality of a child, even if he continued to take the greatest pleasure in the things that children like; nor would anyone choose to find enjoyment in doing something very disgraceful, even if there were no prospect of painful consequences. Besides, there are many things that we should be eager to have even if they brought no pleasure with them – e.g. sight, memory, knowledge, and the several kinds of excellence. It makes no difference if these are necessarily accompanied by pleasure, because we should choose to have them even if we got no pleasure from them.

It seems clear, then, that pleasure is not the good, and that not every pleasure is desirable; also that there are some pleasures that are desirable in themselves, being superior either in kind or in respect of the sources from which they come. This may be taken as a sufficient account of the views propounded about pleasure and pain.

IV.
Pleasure is not a process

What pleasure is, or what its differentia is, may become more readily apparent if we make a fresh start to our inquiry.

The act of seeing is regarded as complete at any moment of its duration, because it does not lack anything that, realized later, will perfect its specific quality. Now pleasure also seems to be of this nature, because it is a sort of whole, i.e. at no moment in time can one fasten upon a pleasure the prolongation of which will enable its specific quality to be perfected. For this reason pleasure is not a process; because every process is in time, and has an end (e.g. the process of building) and is complete when it has accomplished its object. Thus it is complete either in the whole of the time that it takes or at the instant of reaching its end. The particular processes that take place in the parts of this time are all incomplete, and different in kind from the whole and from one another. For example, the fitting together of the stone blocks is different from the fluting of a column, and both are different from the construction of the temple as a whole. This last is a complete process (because nothing further is needed to finish the project); but the building of the base, and the carving of the triglyphs, are incomplete, because each is concerned with a part. Therefore they are different in kind, and it is impossible to fasten upon a specifically complete process at any moment: this is found, if at all, in the whole period of time. Similarly also in the case of walking and so on; for if locomotion is a process of moving from one point to another, there are different species of this too – flying, walking, jumping, etc.; and not only so, but also in walking itself (for the starting and finishing points are not the same in the whole running-track as they are in a part of it, or the same in one part as in another; nor is traversing *this* line the same as traversing *that* one; because the runner does not merely cross *a* line but a line in a certain place; and *this* line is in a different place from *that* one). We have discussed motion in detail elsewhere. It appears, however, that a movement is not complete at any given time; the several movements are incomplete, and differ in kind, since the terminal points constitute specific differences. The form of pleasure, on the other hand, is complete at any given moment.

It is obvious, then, that pleasure and motion are two different things, and that pleasure is something that is whole and complete. This might be concluded also from the fact that a movement must occupy time, whereas a feeling of pleasure does not; for that which is instantaneous is a whole.

These considerations also make it clear that it is wrong to speak of pleasure as a movement or process; for this description does not apply to everything; only to things that are not wholes but consist of parts. Seeing, a point, a unit – none of these is the result of a process (nor is any of them a movement or a process); therefore neither is pleasure, because it is a whole.

The relation of pleasure to activity

Each of the senses is active relatively to its object, and its activity is perfect when it is in a good condition and is directed towards the highest object that falls within its range of sensation. (Something like this seems to be the best description of perfect activity; we may assume that it makes no difference whether we speak of the sense itself, or of the organ in which it resides, as being active.) Therefore the activity of any sense is at its best when the organ is in the best condition and directed towards the best of the objects proper to that sense. This activity will be most perfect and most pleasurable; for there is a pleasure corresponding to each of the senses, just as there is to thought and contemplation; and it is most pleasurable when it is most perfect, and most perfect when the organ is in a healthy condition and directed towards the worthiest of its objects; and the pleasure perfects the activity. It does not, however, perfect it in the same way as the object of the sense and the sense-faculty perfect it when they are good;

just as it is not in the same way that health and the doctor are both causes of one's being healthy.

That each of the senses has its corresponding pleasure is obvious, because we say that sights and sounds are pleasant. It is also obvious that the pleasure is keenest when the sensory faculty is at its best, and exercised upon the best object; when both object and organ are at their best, there will always be pleasure so long as there is something to produce it and someone to feel it. The pleasure perfects the activity not as the formed state that issues in that activity perfects it, by being immanent in it, but as a sort of supervening perfection, like the bloom that graces the flower of youth. So long, then, as the object of thought or sensation, and that which judges or contemplates, are in the right condition, the activity will have its pleasure; for when both subject and object are unchanged and in the same relation to one another, the same result naturally follows.

How is it, then, that nobody feels pleasure continuously? The cause is probably fatigue. No human faculty can be continuously active, so pleasure is not continuous, because it depends upon the activity. Some things please us while they are novelties, but not so much afterwards, for the same reason. At first the mind is stimulated and exercises itself vigorously upon the object, just as people focus their attention in the case of sight; but later the activity declines in vigour and interest is lost; and consequently the pleasure also grows faint.

Pleasure is essential to life

One may suppose that everyone feels drawn towards pleasure, because everyone is eager to live. Life is a form of activity, and each individual directs his activity to those objects, and by means of those faculties, that he likes best: e.g. the musician occupies himself with the sounds of music by the use of his hearing, and the student with the objects of study by the use of his intellect, and similarly with all the other examples. The pleasure perfects the activities, and so perfects life, to which all are drawn. It is quite reasonable, then, that they should also be eager for pleasure; because it perfects life for each individual, and life is a thing to choose. Whether we choose life on account of pleasure or pleasure on account of life is a question that may be dismissed at the moment; for it appears that they are closely connected and do not admit of separation: as pleasure does not occur without activity, so every activity is perfected by its pleasure.

v.

As activities differ in kind, so do their pleasures

This affords ground for the view that pleasures also differ in kind. For we assume that things that are different in kind are perfected by things that are different in kind. This is clearly the case with both natural products like animals and trees, and artificial ones like a picture, a statue, a house or a piece of furniture; and we assume that, similarly, what perfects one kind of activity must differ in kind from what perfects another. But the activities of the intellect differ in kind from those of the senses, and both differ among themselves; therefore so do the pleasures that perfect them.

This can also be seen from the close connection of each pleasure with the activity that it perfects. For the pleasure proper to an activity intensifies it; because those who work with pleasure show better judgement and greater precision in dealing with each class of object: e.g. those who enjoy geometry become good at it and understand its various aspects better, and similarly those who like music or building, and all the other occupations, improve in their proper function if they enjoy it. Thus pleasures intensify their activities; and what intensifies a thing is proper to it; and things that are proper to things that are different in kind are themselves different in kind.

This may be seen still more clearly from the fact that activities are hindered by pleasures derived from other activities. Thus flute-lovers are incapable of attending to a discussion if they catch the sound of somebody playing the flute, because they enjoy the sound of flute-playing more than their immediate activity; so their pleasure in the flute-playing destroys their active participation in the discussion. A similar result follows in all other cases when a person is engaged in two activities at the same time. The more pleasurable activity interferes with the other, and if it is much more pleasurable, does so increasingly, so that the other activity ceases altogether. Hence if we are greatly enjoying anything we do not effectively do something else; and when we are only mildly interested in one occupation we turn to another: e.g. people who chew sweets in the theatre do it most when the acting is poor. And since our activities are concentrated and prolonged and improved by their proper pleasures, and impaired by the pleasures of other activities, it is clear that the two kinds of pleasure differ widely. Indeed alien pleasures have practically the same effect as proper pains, because the proper pains are destructive of the activity; e.g. if a person finds writing or calculating disagreeable and irksome, one man gives up writing and the other calculating, because the activity is painful to him. So activities are affected in opposite ways by their proper pleasures and pains, 'proper' meaning those that become attached to the activity in virtue of itself. Alien pleasures, as we have said, have an effect very close to that of pain, because they are destructive, only not to the same degree.

Since activities differ in goodness and badness, and some are to be chosen, some to be avoided and some neutral, their pleasures can be classed similarly, because each activity has a pleasure proper to it. Thus the pleasure proper to a serious activity is virtuous, and that which is proper to a bad one is vicious; for desires too are laudable if their objects are noble, but censurable if they are base. The pleasures involved in activities are more proper to them than the impulses that arouse them, because the latter are differentiated from the activities both by their nature and by the time at which they occur, whereas the pleasures are closely connected with them, and so little distinguishable that it is disputable whether the activity and its pleasure are the same or not. Not that there is any real ground for supposing that the pleasure *is* thinking or sensating (for that would be absurd); but because they are inseparable they appear to some to be identical.

The pleasures, then, are as diverse as their activities. Sight is superior to touch, and hearing and smell to taste, in purity, so their pleasures differ similarly. Also intellectual pleasures are superior to sensuous ones, and both kinds differ among themselves.

It is thought that every animal has a proper pleasure, just as it has a proper function: namely, the pleasure of exercising that function. This will be clear if one considers individual species; because a horse, a dog and a man each have a different pleasure, as Heraclitus says that a donkey would prefer sweepings to gold, because they are nicer for a donkey to eat.

Different species of animals, then, have different kinds of pleasures, but it would be reasonable for the pleasures to be uniform within the same species. However, in the case of human beings at any rate, they show no little divergence. The same things delight one set of people and annoy another; what is painful and detestable to some is pleasurable and likeable to others. This happens in the case of sweet things too: they do not taste the same to a feverish patient as they do to a normal person; nor does the same thing seem hot to an invalid and to a man in perfect health. The same sort of thing happens in other cases too.

Only the good man's pleasures are real and truly human

But in all such circumstances it is generally accepted that the good man's view is the true one. If this formula is correct, as it seems to be; that is, if the standard by which we measure everything is goodness, or the good man *qua* good: then the true pleasures too will be those that seem to him to be pleasures, and those things will be really pleasant that he enjoys. And if things that displease him seem pleasant to somebody else, it is not at all surprising; for humanity is subject to many kinds of corruption and perversion, and the things in question are pleasant only to these persons in their particular condition. Clearly, then, we must deny that the admittedly disreputable pleasures are pleasures at all, except to the depraved; but of those that are regarded as reputable which, or what sort, should we pronounce to be the pleasure of man? Probably this will emerge from a study of human activities, because these are attended by their proper pleasures. So whether the perfect and supremely happy man has one activity or more than one, it is the pleasures that perfect these that can properly be described as *human*; the remainder, like their activities, can be so called only in a secondary or far lower degree.

VI.
Recapitulation: the nature of happiness

Now that we have finished our discussion of the virtues, of friendship and of pleasures, it remains for us to give an outline account of happiness, since we hold it to be the end of human conduct. It may make our treatment of the subject more concise if we recapitulate what has been said already.

We said, then, that happiness is not a *state*, since if it were it might belong even to a man who slept all through his life, passing a vegetable existence; or to a victim of the greatest misfortunes. So if this is unacceptable, and we ought rather to refer happiness to some activity, as we said earlier; and if activities are either necessary and to be chosen for the sake of something else, or to be chosen for themselves: clearly we must class happiness as one of those to be chosen for themselves, and not as one of the other kind, because it does not need anything else: it is self-sufficient. The activities that are to be chosen for themselves are those from which nothing is required beyond the exercise of the activity; and such a description is thought to fit actions that accord with goodness; because the doing of fine and good actions is one of the things that are to be chosen for themselves.

Happiness must be distinguished from amusement

Pleasant amusements are also thought to belong to this class, because they are not chosen as means to something else: in fact their effects are more harmful than beneficial, since they

make people neglect their bodies and their property. However, most of those who are regarded as happy have recourse
to such occupations, and that is why those who show some
dexterity in them are highly esteemed at the courts of tyrants;
they make themselves agreeable by providing the sort of
entertainment that their patrons want, and such persons are
in demand. So these amusements are thought to be conducive to happiness, because men in positions of power devote
their leisure to them. But what people of this kind do is probably no evidence, because virtue and intelligence, which are
the sources of serious activities, do not depend upon positions
of power; and if these persons, never having tasted pure and
refined pleasure, have recourse to physical pleasures, that is
no reason why the latter should be regarded as worthier of
choice. Children, too, believe that the things they prize are
the most important; so it is natural that just as different things
seem valuable to children and adults, so they should seem
different also to good and bad men. Thus, as we have often
said, it is the things that seem valuable and pleasant to the
good man that are really such. But to each individual it is the
activity in accordance with his own disposition that is most
desirable, and therefore to the good man virtuous activity is
most desirable. It follows that happiness does not consist in
amusement. Indeed it would be paradoxical if the end were
amusement; if we toiled and suffered all our lives long
to amuse ourselves. For we choose practically everything for
the sake of something else, except happiness, because it is the
end. To spend effort and toil for the sake of amusement seems
silly and unduly childish; but on the other hand the maxim
of Anacharsis, 'Play to work harder', seems to be on the right
lines, because amusement is a form of relaxation, and people
need relaxation because they cannot exert themselves

continuously. Therefore relaxation is not an end, because it is taken for the sake of the activity. But the happy life seems to be lived in accordance with goodness, and such a life implies seriousness and does not consist in amusing oneself. Also we maintain that serious things are better than those that are merely comical and amusing, and that the activity of a man, or part of a man, is always more serious in proportion as it is better. Therefore the activity of the better part is superior, and *eo ipso* more conducive to happiness.

Anybody can enjoy bodily pleasures – a slave no less than the best of men – but nobody attributes a part in happiness to a slave, unless he also attributes to him a life of his own. Therefore happiness does not consist in occupations of this kind, but in activities in accordance with virtue, as we have said before.

VII.
Happiness and contemplation

If happiness is an activity in accordance with virtue, it is reasonable to assume that it is in accordance with the highest virtue, and this will be the virtue of the best part of us. Whether this is the intellect or something else that we regard as naturally ruling and guiding us, and possessing insight into things noble and divine – either as being actually divine itself or as being more divine than any other part of us – it is the activity of this part, in accordance with the virtue proper to it, that will be perfect happiness.

We have already said that it is a contemplative activity. This may be regarded as consonant both with our earlier arguments and with the truth. For contemplation is both the highest form of activity (since the intellect is the highest thing in us, and the objects that it apprehends are the highest things that can be known), and also it is the most continuous, because we are more capable of continuous contemplation than we are of any practical activity. Also we assume that happiness must contain an admixture of pleasure; now activity in accordance with philosophic wisdom is admittedly the most pleasant of the virtuous activities; at any rate philosophy is held to entail pleasures that are marvellous in purity and permanence; and it stands to reason that those who possess knowledge pass their time more pleasantly than those who are still in pursuit of it. Again, the quality that we call self-sufficiency will belong in the highest degree to the contemplative activity. The wise man, no less than the just one and all the rest, requires the necessaries of life; but, given an adequate supply of these, the just man also needs people with and towards whom he can perform just actions, and similarly with the temperate man, the brave man and each of the others; but the wise man can practise contemplation by himself, and the wiser he is, the more he can do it. No doubt he does it better with the help of fellow-workers; but for all that he is the most self-sufficient of men. Again, contemplation would seem to be the only activity that is appreciated for its own sake; because nothing is gained from it except the act of contemplation, whereas from practical activities we expect to gain something more or less over and above the action.

Since happiness is thought to imply leisure, it must be an intellectual, not a practical activity

Also it is commonly believed that happiness depends on leisure; because we occupy ourselves so that we may have leisure, just as we make war in order that we may live at peace. Now the exercise of the practical virtues takes place in politics or in warfare, and these professions seem to have no place for leisure. This is certainly true of the military profession, for nobody chooses to make war or provokes it for the sake of making war; a man would be regarded as a bloodthirsty monster if he made his friends into enemies in order to bring about battles and slaughter. The politician's profession also makes leisure impossible, since besides the business of politics it aims at securing positions of power and honour, or the happiness of the politician himself and of his fellow-citizens – a happiness separate from politics, and one which we clearly pursue as separate.

If, then, politics and warfare, although pre-eminent in nobility and grandeur among practical activities in accordance with goodness, are incompatible with leisure and, not being desirable in themselves, are directed towards some other end, whereas the activity of the intellect is considered to excel in seriousness, taking as it does the form of contemplation, and to aim at no other end beyond itself and to possess a pleasure peculiar to itself, which intensifies its activity; and if it is evident that self-sufficiency and leisuredness and such freedom from fatigue as is humanly possible, together with all the other attributes assigned to the supremely happy man, are those that accord with this activity; then this activity will be the perfect happiness for man – provided that it is allowed a full span of life; for nothing that pertains to happiness is incomplete.

Life on this plane is not too high for the
divine element in human nature

But such a life will be too high for human attainment; for any man who lives it will do so not as a human being but in virtue of something divine within him, and in proportion as this divine element is superior to the composite being, so will its activity be superior to that of the other kind of virtue. So if the intellect is divine compared with man, the life of the intellect must be divine compared with the life of a human being. And we ought not to listen to those who warn us that 'man should think the thoughts of man', or 'mortal thoughts fit mortal minds'; but we ought, so far as in us lies, to put on immortality, and do all that we can to live in conformity with the highest that is in us; for even if it is small in bulk, in power and preciousness it far excels all the rest. Indeed it would seem that this is the true self of the individual, since it is the authoritative and better part of him; so it would be an odd thing if a man chose to live someone else's life instead of his own. Moreover, what we said above will apply here too: that what is best and most pleasant for any given creature is that which is proper to it. Therefore for man, too, the best and most pleasant life is the life of the intellect, since the intellect is in the fullest sense the man. So this life will also be the happiest.

VIII.
Moral activity is secondary happiness

Life in conformity with the other kind of virtue will be happy in a secondary degree, because activities in accordance with it are human. It is in our dealings with one another that we act justly and bravely and display the other virtues, observing what is due to each person in all contracts and mutual services and actions of every kind, and in our feelings too; and all these are obviously *human* experiences. Some of them are even thought to have a physical origin, and moral goodness is considered to be intimately connected in various ways with

the feelings. Prudence, too, is closely linked with moral goodness, and moral goodness with prudence, since the first
principles of prudence are given by the moral virtues, and
the right standard for the virtues is set by prudence. These
moral virtues, being bound up with the feelings too, will also
belong to the composite person. But the virtues of the composite person are human. Therefore the life that conforms
with these virtues, and the happiness that belongs to it, are
also human. But the happiness of the intellect is separate. Let
us leave it at that, because a detailed treatment would exceed
the scope of our present inquiry. It would also seem to stand
in little need of external accessories, or in less need than
moral goodness does. We may assume that both require the
necessities of life, and in equal measure (although the politician spends more effort on the provision of bodily needs and
the like), because in this respect there may be little difference
between them; but there will be a vast difference in what
they require for their activities. The liberal man will need
money to perform liberal acts, as indeed will the just man to
meet his obligations (for intentions do not show, and even
the unjust pretend that they wish to act justly); the brave man
will need potency if he is to achieve anything valorous, and
the temperate man will need opportunity; for how else can
he, or any other virtuous person, display his quality?

It is disputed whether the intention or the actions have
the greater importance in determining the goodness of conduct, assuming that it depends on both. Well, its perfection
would clearly involve both, and for the performance of virtuous actions many accessories are required, and the grander
and nobler the actions the more numerous will these accessories be. On the other hand the contemplative has no need
of such things for his activity; on the contrary they are almost

a hindrance to his contemplation. However, in so far as he is a human being and a member of society he chooses to act in accordance with virtue; therefore he will need external goods to enable him to live as a human being.

The view that happiness is contemplation is confirmed by other arguments

That perfect happiness is a kind of contemplative activity may be shown also from the following argument. The gods in our conception of them are supremely happy and blessed, but what kind of actions should we attribute to them? If we say 'Just actions', surely we shall be confronted by the absurdity of their making contracts and returning deposits and all that sort of thing. Well, shall we say 'Brave actions' – facing terrors and risking their persons in the cause of honour? What of liberal actions? They will have nobody to give to; and it is absurd that they should actually have coined money or its equivalent. What form could their temperate actions take? Surely it would be cheap praise, since they have no evil desires! If we went through the whole list we should find that the practical details of these actions are petty and unworthy of gods. On the other hand men have always conceived of them as at least living beings, and therefore active; for we cannot suppose that they spend their time in sleeping, like Endymion. But if a living being is deprived of action, and still further of production, what is left but contemplation? It follows, then, that the activity of the gods, which is supremely happy, must be a form of contemplation; and therefore among human activities that which is most akin to the gods' will be the happiest.

This view is further supported by the fact that the lower animals have no share in happiness, being completely incapable of such an activity. The life of the gods is altogether happy, and that of man is happy in so far as it contains something that resembles the divine activity; but none of the lower animals is happy, because they have no way of participating in contemplation. Happiness, then, is co-extensive with contemplation, and the more people contemplate, the happier they are; not incidentally, but in virtue of their contemplation, because it is in itself precious. Thus happiness is a form of contemplation.

But its possessor, being only human, will also need external felicity, because human nature is not self-sufficient for the purpose of contemplation; the body too must be healthy, and food and other amenities must be available. On the other hand it must not be supposed that, because one cannot be happy without external goods, it will be necessary to have many of them on a grand scale in order to be happy at all. For self-sufficiency does not depend upon a superfluity of means, nor does moral conduct; and it is possible to perform fine acts even if one is not master of land and sea. Indeed, a man can conduct himself virtuously even from a modest competence (this can be quite plainly seen, for private persons are considered to perform decent actions not less but actually more than those who are in positions of power). It is enough, then, to possess this much; for a man's life will be happy if he acts in accordance with virtue. Solon, too, was presumably right in his description of happy people when he said that they were those who were moderately equipped with external goods, and had achieved what were, as he thought, the finest deeds and had lived temperate lives; for it is possible for those who have only moderate possessions to do what is right. Anaxagoras, too, seems not to have pictured the happy man as wealthy or powerful when he said that it would not surprise him if such a person were an oddity in most people's eyes, because they judge by outward appearances, which are all that they can perceive. Thus it appears that our arguments are in harmony with the opinions of the wise. Such considerations do indeed carry some conviction; but in the matter of conduct truth is assessed in the light of the facts and of actual life; because it is in these that the decisive factor lies. So we must bring what we have already said to the test of the facts of life; and if it accords with the facts, we can accept it, but if it conflicts with them we must regard it as no more than a theory.

The man who exercises his intellect and cultivates it seems likely to be in the best state of mind and to be most loved by the gods. For if, as is generally supposed, the gods have some concern for human affairs, it would be reasonable to believe also that they take pleasure in that part of us which is best and most closely related to themselves (this being the intellect), and that they reward those who appreciate and honour it most highly; for they care for what is dear to them, and what they do is right and good. Now it is not hard to see that it is the wise man that possesses these qualities in the highest degree; therefore he is dearest to the gods. And it is natural that he should also be the happiest of men. So on this score too the wise man will be happy in the highest degree.

IX.
*So much for ethical theory. How can
it be put into practice?*

Assuming, then, that we have given (in outline) a sufficient account of happiness and the several virtues, and also of friendship and pleasure, may we regard our undertaking as now completed? Or is the correct view that (as we have been saying) in the case of conduct the end consists not in gaining theoretical knowledge of the several points at issue, but rather in putting our knowledge into practice? In that case it is not enough to know about goodness; we must endeavour to possess and use it, or adopt any other means to become good ourselves. Now if discourses were enough in themselves to make people moral, to quote Theognis 'Many and fat would be the fees they earned', quite rightly; and to provide such discourses would be what is needed. But as it is we find that although they have the power to stimulate and encourage those of the young who are liberal-minded, and although they can render a generous and truly idealistic character susceptible of virtue, they are incapable of impelling the masses towards human perfection. For it is the nature of the many to be ruled by fear rather than by shame, and to refrain from evil not because of the disgrace but because of the punishments. Living under the sway of their feelings, they pursue their own pleasures and the means of obtaining them, and shun the pains that are their opposites; but of that which is fine and truly pleasurable they have not even a conception, since they have never had a taste of it. What discourse could ever reform people like that? To dislodge by argument habits long embedded in the character is a difficult if not impossible task. We should probably be content if the combination of all the means that are supposed to make us good enables us to attain some portion of goodness.

Goodness can only be induced in
a suitably receptive character

Some thinkers hold that it is by nature that people become good, others that it is by habit and others that it is by instruction.

The bounty of nature is clearly beyond our control; it is bestowed by some divine dispensation upon those who are truly fortunate. It is a regrettable fact that discussion and instruction are not effective in all cases; just as a piece of land has to be prepared beforehand if it is to nourish the seed, so the mind of the pupil has to be prepared in its habits if it is to enjoy and dislike the right things; because the man who lives in accordance with his feelings would not listen to an argument to dissuade him, or understand it if he did. And when a man is in that state, how is it possible to persuade him out of it? In general, feeling seems to yield not to argument but only to force. Therefore we must have a character to work on that has some affinity to virtue: one that appreciates what is noble and objects to what is base.

Education in goodness is best undertaken by the state

But to obtain a right training for goodness from an early age is a hard thing, unless one has been brought up under right laws. For a temperate and hardy way of life is not a pleasant thing to most people, especially when they are young. For this reason upbringing and occupations should be regulated by law, because they will cease to be irksome when they have become habitual. But presumably it is not enough to have received the right upbringing and supervision in youth; they must keep on observing their regimen and accustoming themselves to it even after they are grown up; so we shall need laws to regulate these activities too, and indeed generally to cover the whole of life; for most people are readier to submit to compulsion and punishment than to argument and fine ideals. This is why some people think that although legislators ought to encourage people to goodness and appeal to their finer feelings, in the hope that those who have had a decent training in their habits will respond, they ought also to inflict chastisement and penalties on any who disobey through deficiency of character, and to deport the incorrigible altogether. For they hold that while the good man, whose life is related to a fine ideal, will listen to reason, the bad one whose object is pleasure must be controlled by pain, like a beast of burden. This is also why they say that the pains inflicted should be those that are most contrary to the favoured pleasures.

To resume, however: if (as we have said) in order to be a good man one must first have been brought up in the right way and trained in the right habits, and must thereafter spend one's life in reputable occupations, doing no wrong either with or against one's will: then this can be achieved by living under the guidance of some intelligence or right system that has effective force. Now the orders that a father gives have no forceful or compulsive power, nor indeed have those of any individual in general, unless he is a king or somebody of that sort; but law, being the pronouncement of a kind of practical wisdom or intelligence, does have the power of compulsion. And although people resent it when their impulses are opposed by human agents, even if the latter are in the right, the law causes no irritation by enjoining decent behaviour. Yet in Sparta alone, or almost alone, the lawgiver seems to have concerned himself with upbringing and daily life. In the great majority of states matters of this kind have been completely neglected, and every man lives his life as he likes, 'laying down the law for wife and children', like the Cyclopes.

*If neglected by the state, it can be supplied
by the parent; but it calls for some knowledge
of legislative science*

The best solution would be to introduce a proper system of
public supervision of these matters. But if they continue to
be completely neglected by the state, it would seem to be
right for each individual to help his own children and friends
on the way to goodness, and that he should have the power
or at least the choice of doing this. And it would seem from
what we have said that he will be better able to do it if he
assumes the role of legislator. For obviously public control is
carried out by means of laws, and if the control is good, by
means of sound laws; but whether they are written or unwrit-
ten, whether they are to regulate the education of one person
or of many, would seem to matter no more than in the case
of music or physical education or any other subject of study.
The instruction and habits prescribed by a father have as
much force in the household as laws and customs have in the
state, and even more, because of the tie of blood and the
children's sense of benefits received; for they are influenced
from the outset by natural affection and docility. Moreover,
individual tuition, like individual treatment in medicine, is
actually superior to the public sort. For example, as a general
rule rest and fasting are beneficial in a case of fever, but not,
perhaps, for a particular patient; and presumably a boxing
instructor does not make all his pupils adopt the same manner of fighting. It would seem, then, that particular cases
receive more accurate treatment when individual attention
is given, because then each person is more likely to get what

suits him. But the best detailed treatment will be given by the doctor (or trainer or any other instructor) who has a general knowledge of what is good for all cases, or for a specific type; because the sciences not only are said to be but are concerned with common facts. This is not to deny that in a particular case it is probably quite possible for the right treatment to be given by one who has no knowledge, but has carefully observed (in the course of his experience) the effects upon individuals of different kinds of treatment; just as some people really seem to be their own best doctors, although they would be quite unable to help anybody else. Nevertheless it would presumably be agreed that anyone who wants to be professionally qualified with theoretical knowledge must proceed to the study of the universal and get to know it as well as possible; for it is with this (as we have said) that the sciences deal. Probably, then, one who wishes to make other people (whether many or few) better by supervision ought first to try to acquire the art of legislation; assuming that we can be made good by laws. For producing a right disposition in any person that is set before you is not a task for everybody: if anyone can do it, it is the man with knowledge – just as in the case of medicine and all the other professions that call for application and practical understanding.

Where can such knowledge be obtained? *Not from the sophists*

Surely, then, the next question to consider is from whom or by what means one can acquire a grasp of legislation. Presumably, as in the case of the other sciences, from the politicians; because legislation is regarded, as we saw, as a branch of political science. But it seems that the case is perhaps not the same with political science as it is with the rest of the sciences and faculties. In all the others we find the same persons both putting their skills into practice and imparting them to others; e.g. doctors and painters. But as for political science, although the sophists profess to teach it, not one of them practises it; that is done by the politicians, and they would seem to do it from a sort of ability aided by experience rather than by the exercise of reason. For we do not find them writing or lecturing about political subjects (although this would perhaps be more to their credit than composing speeches for the law courts or public meetings); nor again do we find that they have made politicians out of their sons or anyone else that they care for. And yet that would have been their logical course, if they were capable of it. For they could not have left a finer legacy to their countries, nor is there anything that they would rather have had for themselves, and therefore for those dearest to them, than that sort of ability. At the same time experience seems to contribute not a little to success in politics, for otherwise people would never have become statesmen through familiarity with political problems. So it seems that those who aspire to a scientific knowledge of politics need practical experience as well.

On the other hand those sophists who profess to teach politics seem to be very far from actually doing so. They are in fact absolutely ignorant both of the nature of the subject and of the matters with which it deals; otherwise they would not equate it with, or rate it even lower than, rhetoric. Nor would they imagine that it is easy to frame a constitution by making a collection of the laws that have been most highly approved, because then you can select the best of them – as if the actual selection did not call for understanding, and as if a correct judgement were not the crucial factor, just as it is in musical questions. It is only the experts in a given art who can judge its products correctly and understand by what means and methods perfection is achieved, and which elements can be harmoniously combined; amateurs may be content if they do not remain unaware whether the result is good or bad, as in the case of painting. Laws represent the products of the art of politics: how then can a collection of laws teach a man the art of legislation, or help him to pick out the best of them? We do not find people becoming qualified in medicine by reading handbooks, although the authors at least attempt to describe not only general methods of treatment but also possible methods of cure and proper modes of treatment for each type of patient, classifying them by their bodily states; and these handbooks are considered to be helpful to the experienced, but useless to the layman. Presumably, then, collections of laws and constitutions may be serviceable to those who are capable of examining them critically and judging what is rightly enacted and what is the opposite, and what sort of legislation is suitable for different circumstances. But those who go through such collections of examples without possessing a formed habit of mind, although they cannot assess merit correctly, except by a kind of instinct, may perhaps improve their understanding of the subject.

The student of ethics must therefore apply himself to politics

Since, then, the question of legislation has been left unexamined by previous thinkers, presumably we had better investigate it more closely for ourselves, together with the question of constitutions generally, so that our philosophy of human conduct may be as complete as possible. So let us first try to review any valid statements (about particular points) that have been made by our predecessors; and then to consider, in the light of our collected examples of constitutions, what influences are conservative and what are destructive of a state; and which have these effects upon each different kind of constitution; and for what reasons some states are well governed, while in others the contrary is the case. For after examining these questions we shall perhaps see more comprehensively what kind of constitution is the best, and what is the best organization for each kind and the best system of laws and customs for it to use. Let us, then, begin our account.